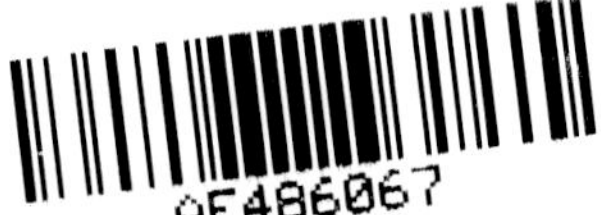

DATE : ....

NAME   : ....

AGE   : ....

CITY   : ....

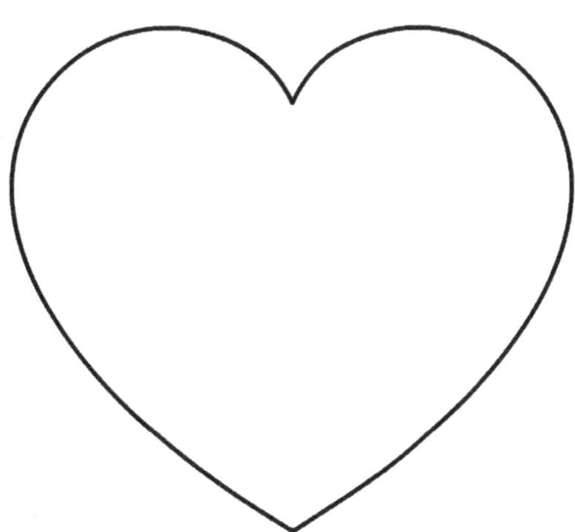

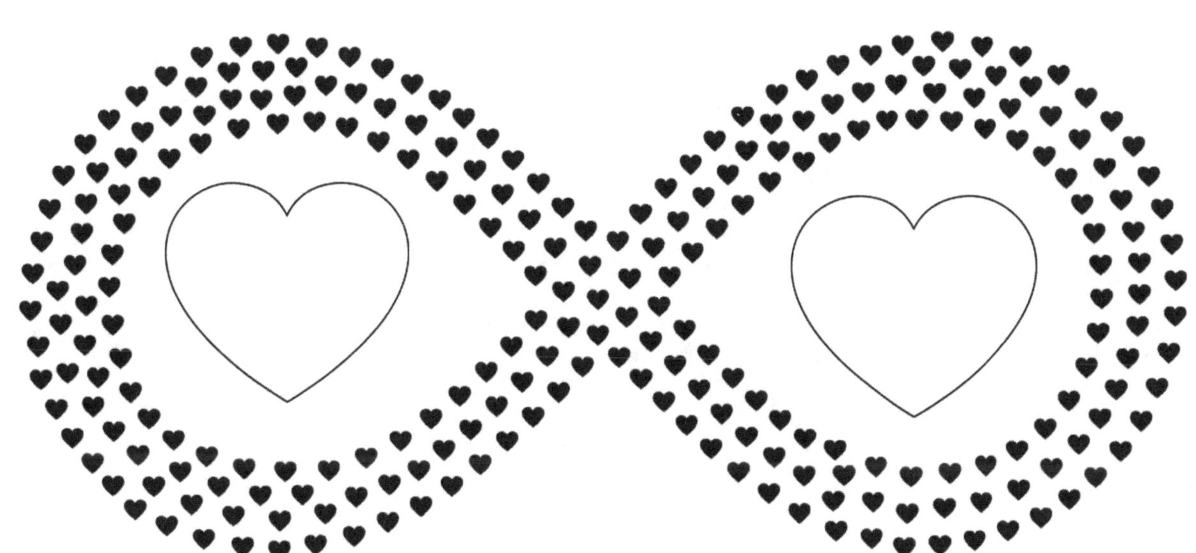

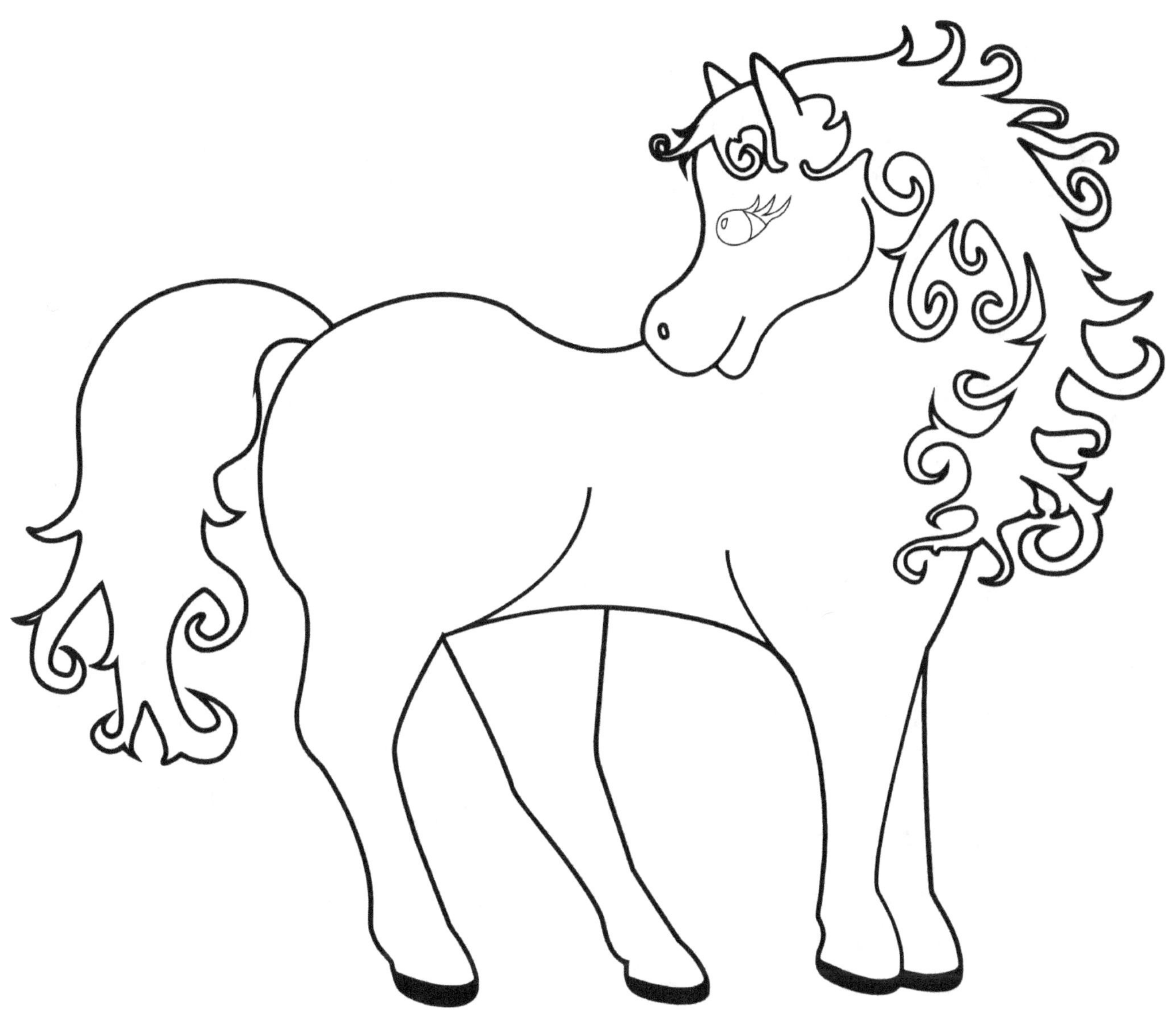

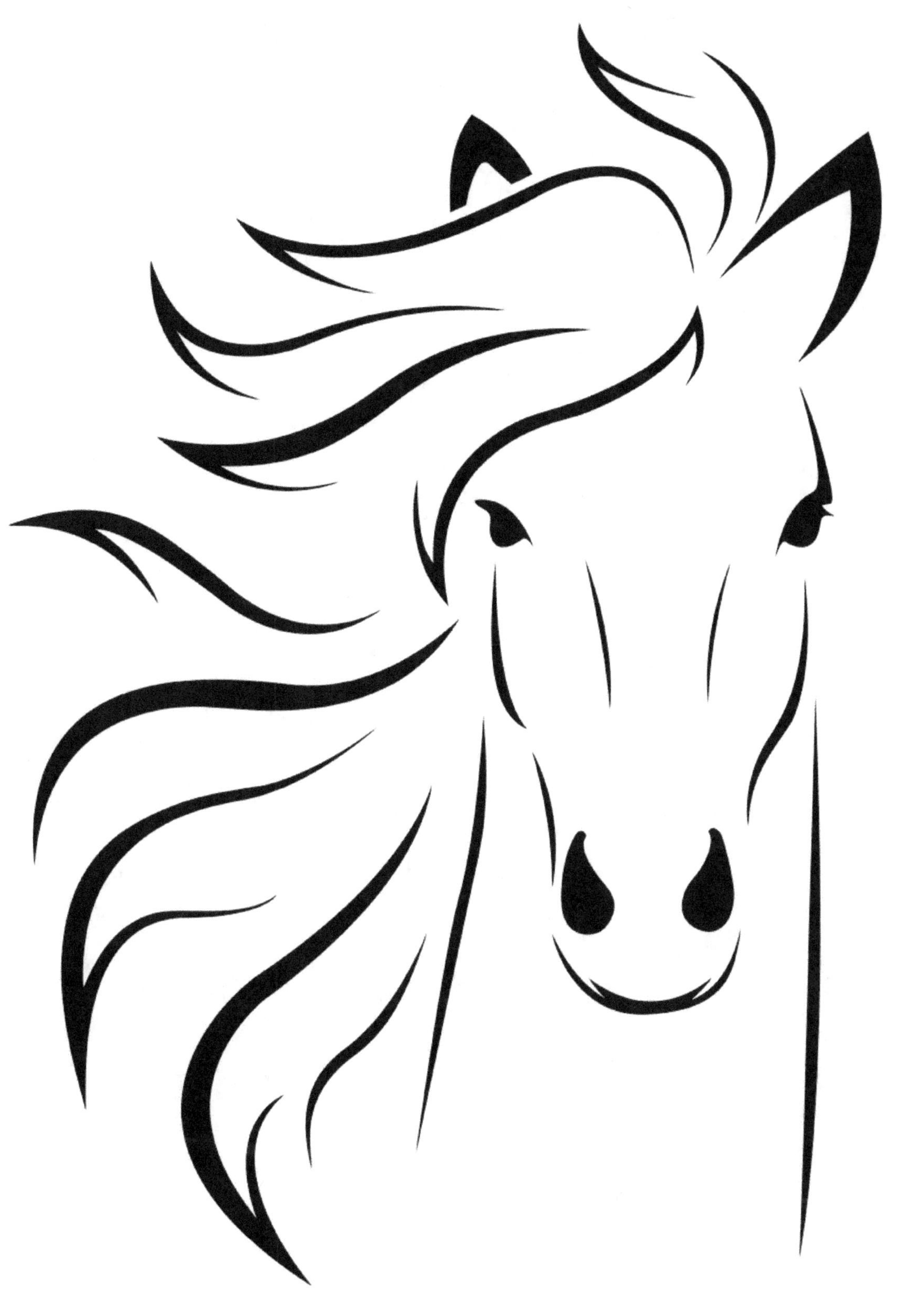

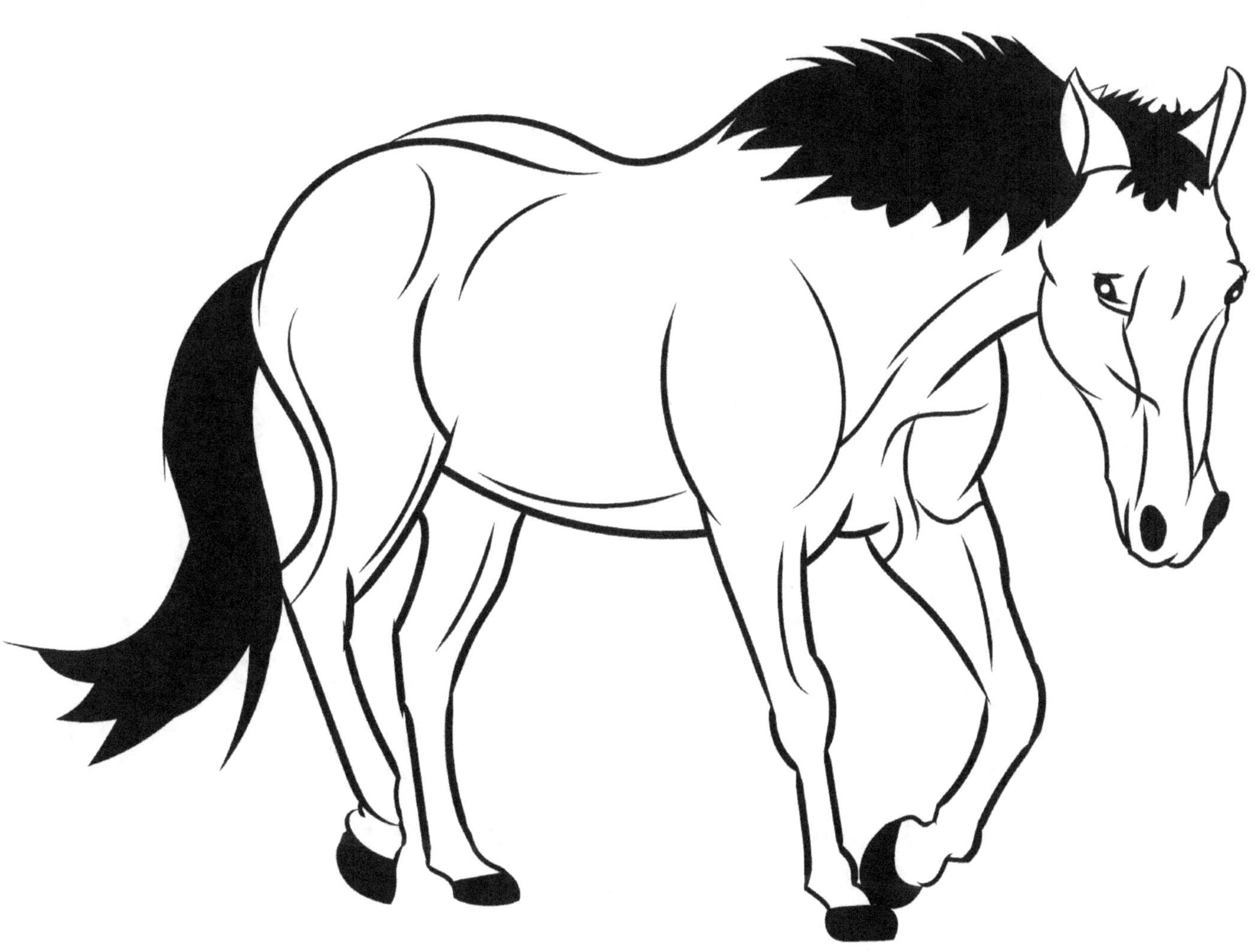

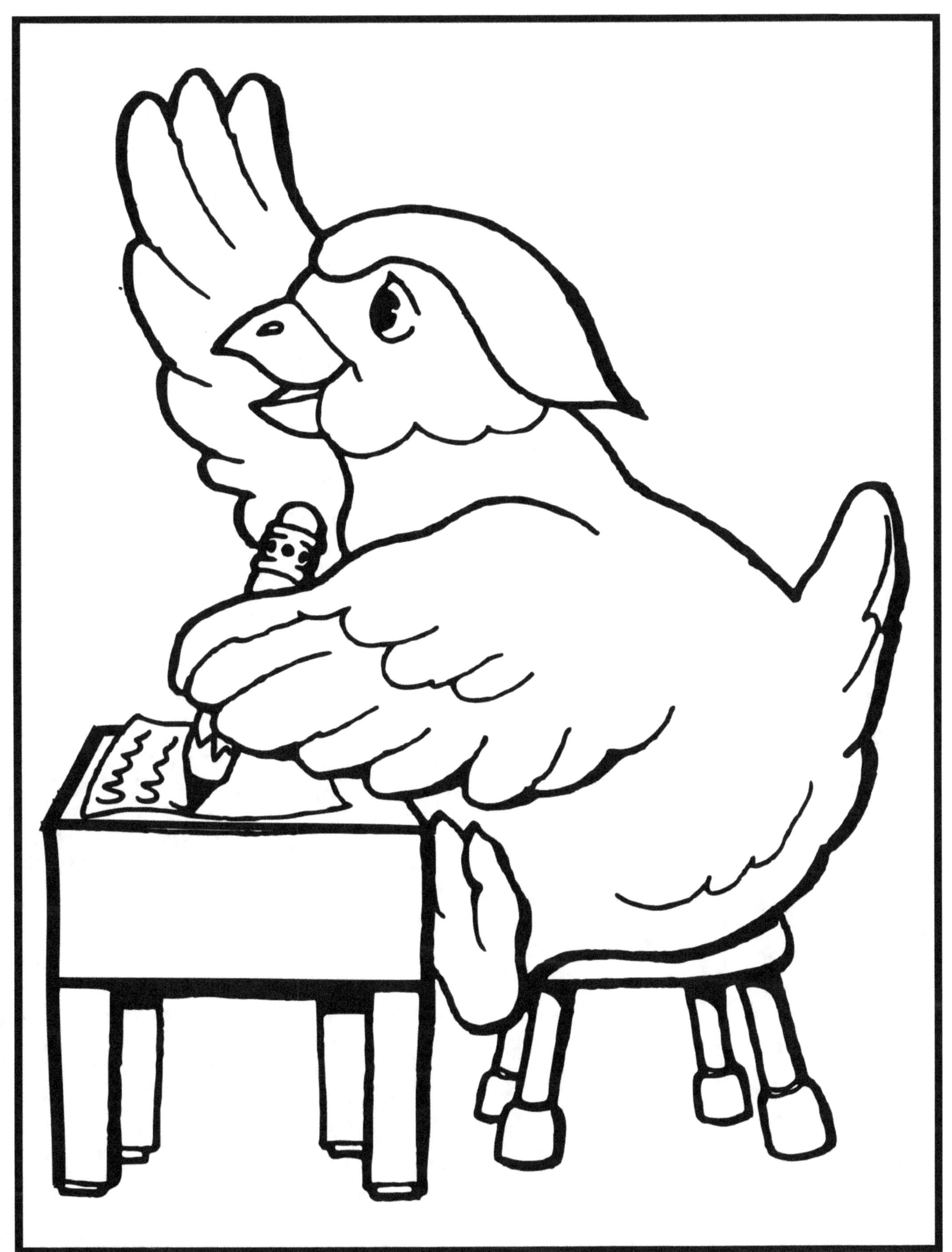

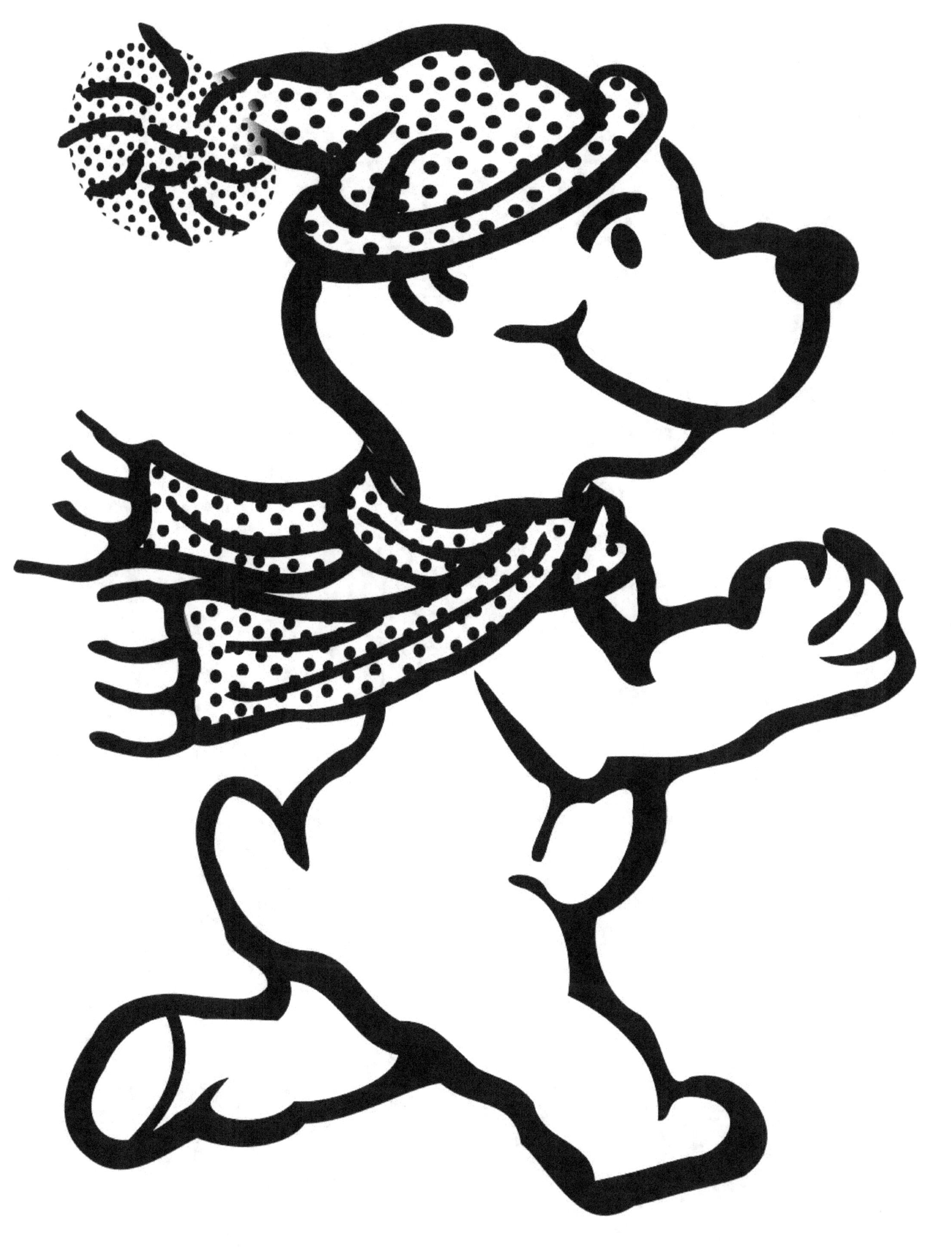

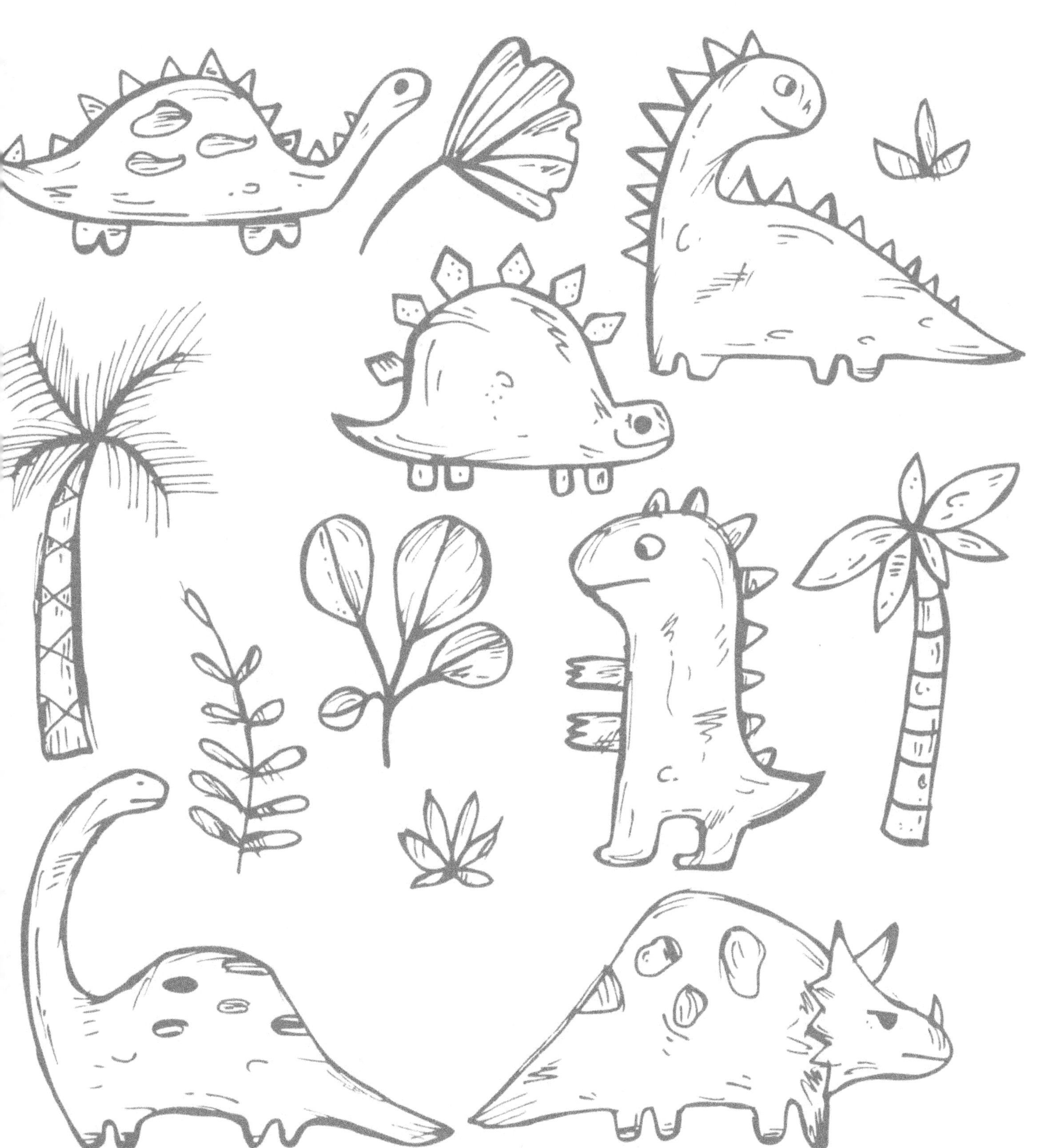

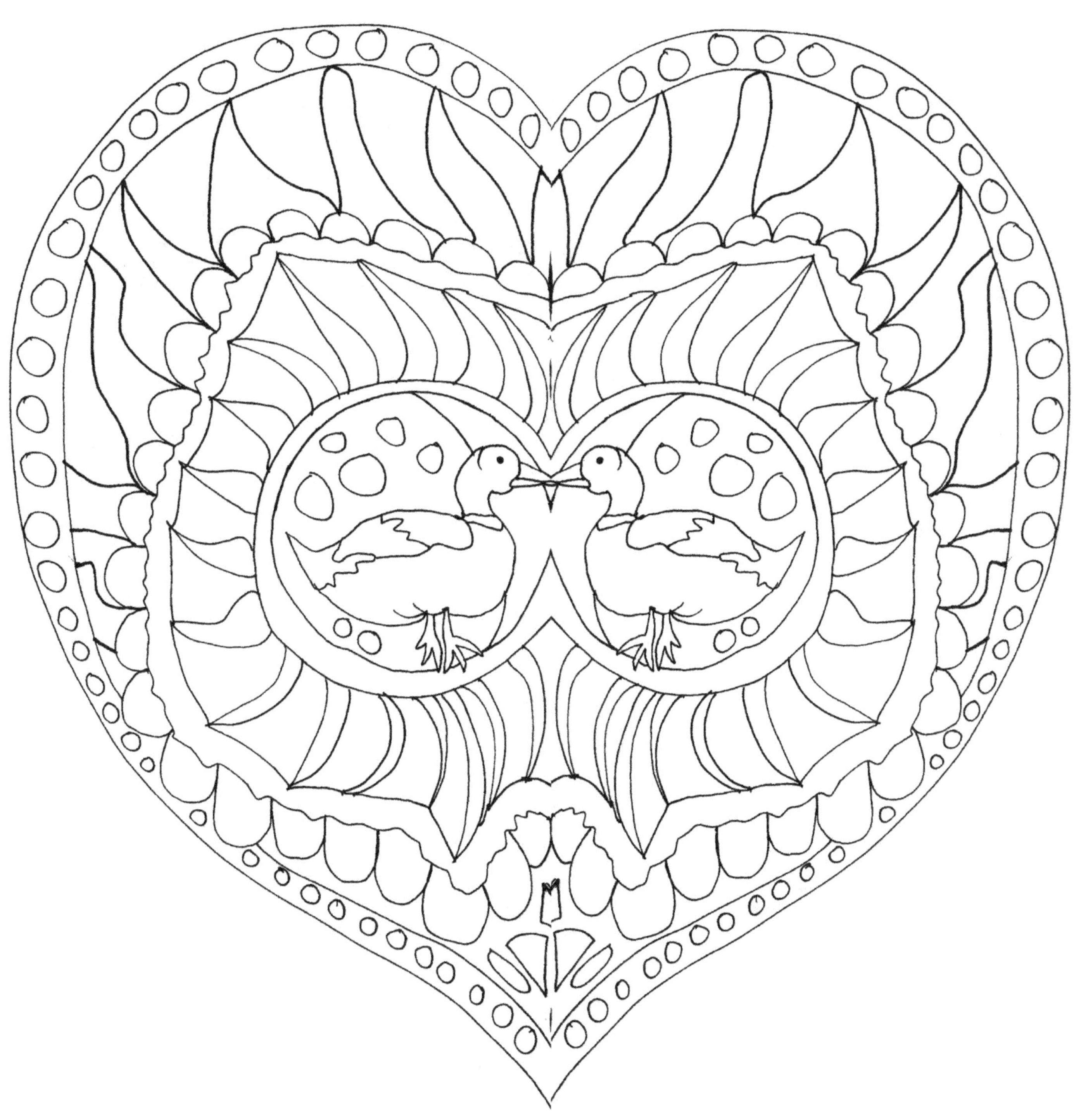

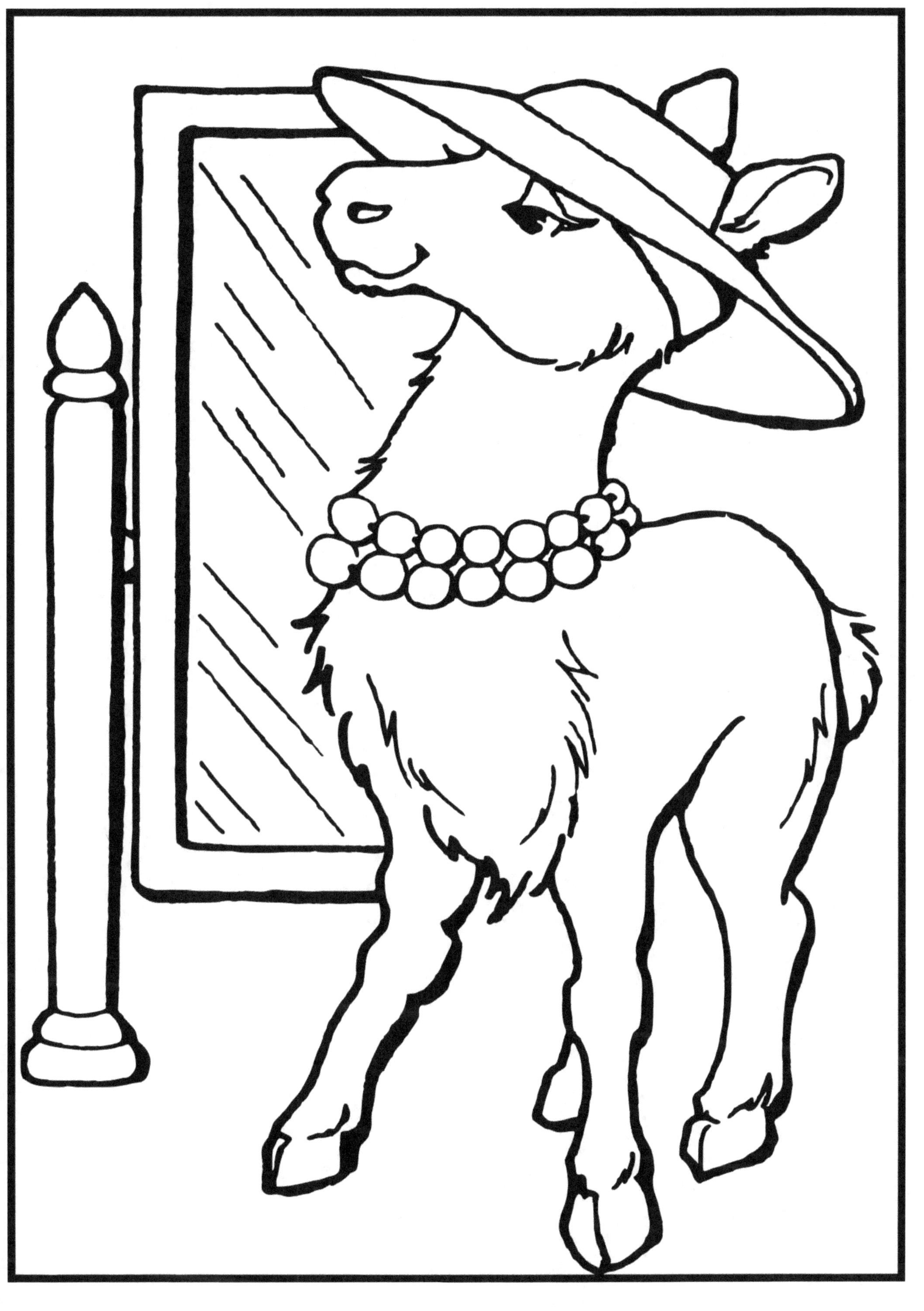

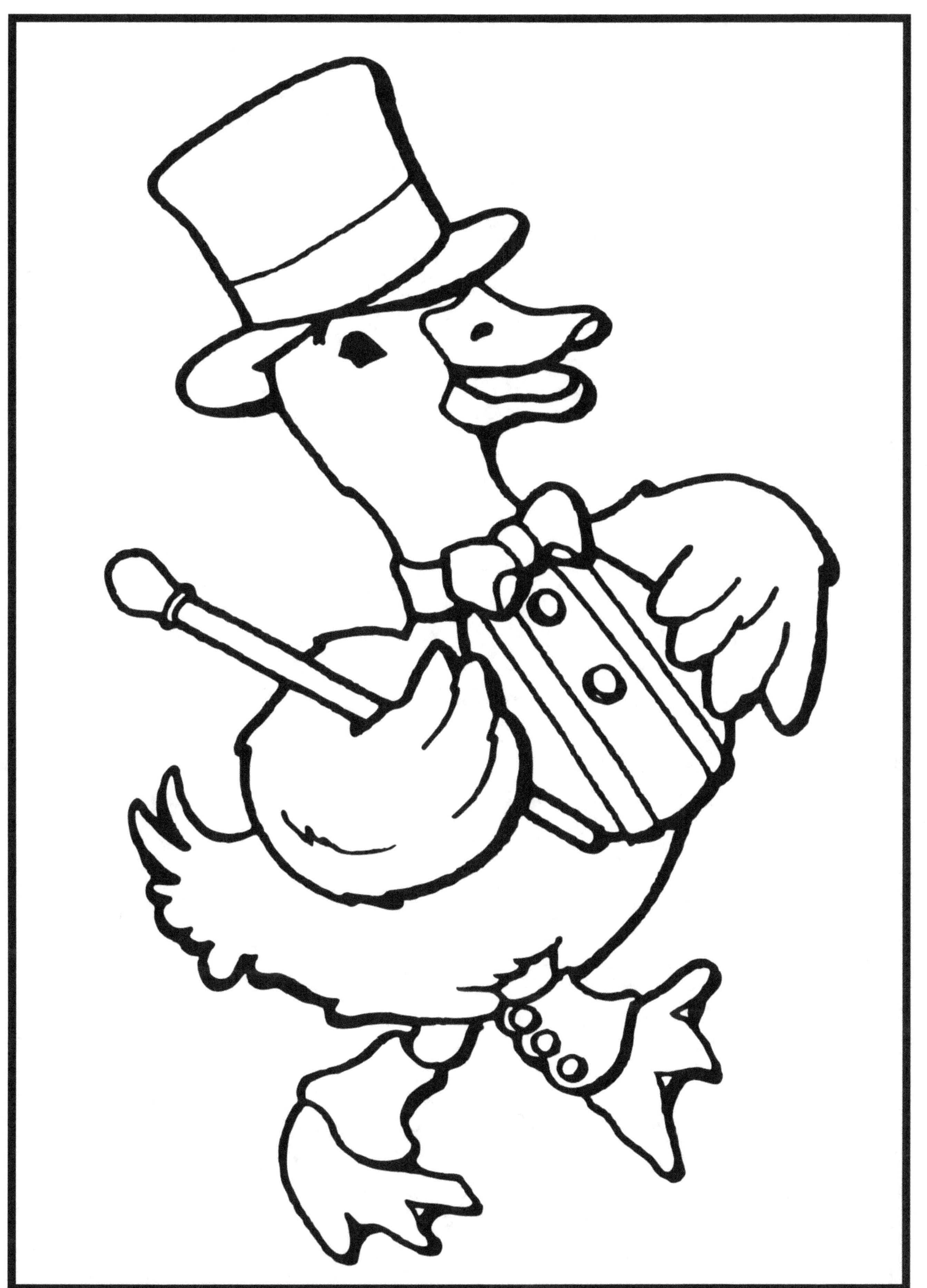

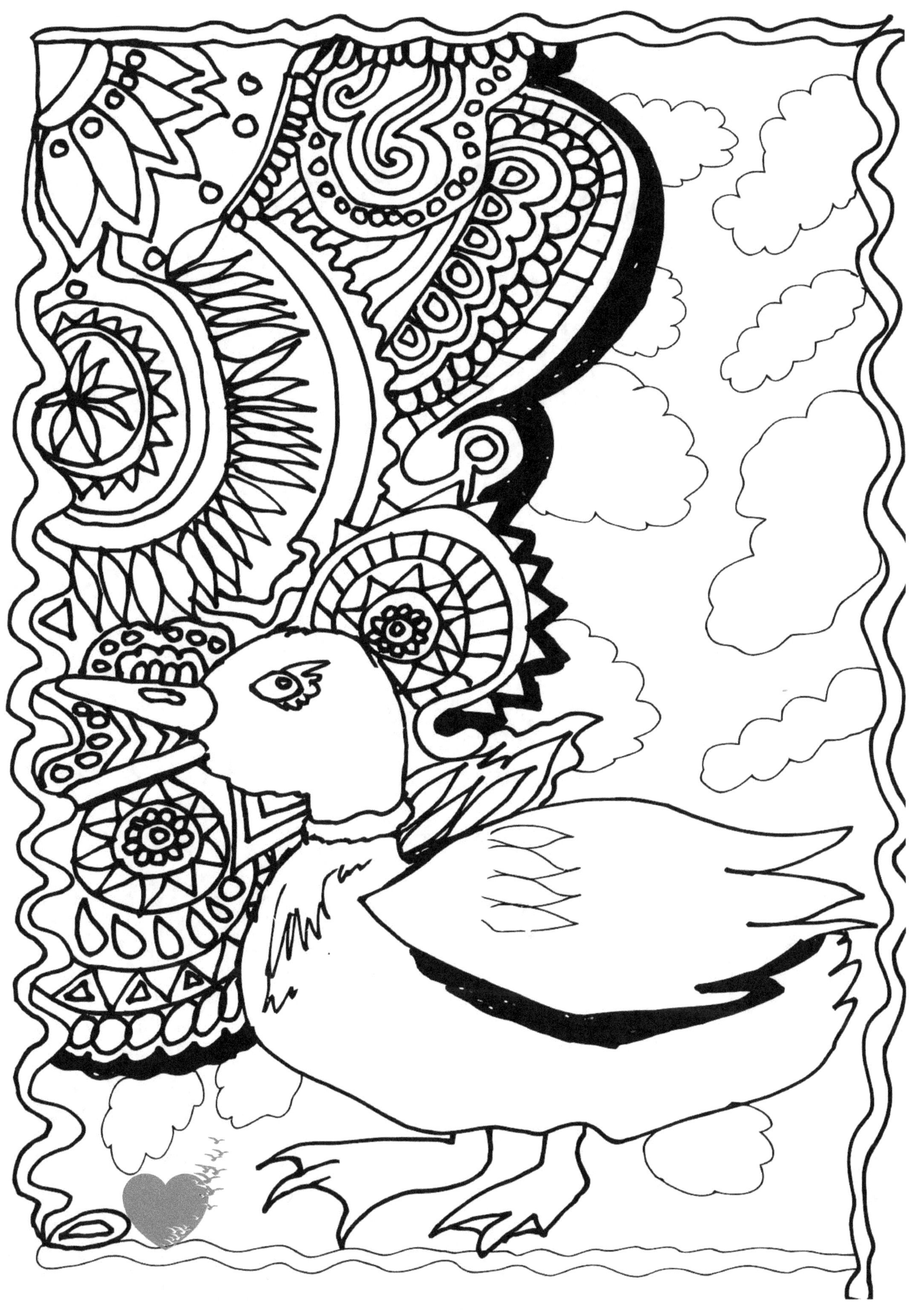

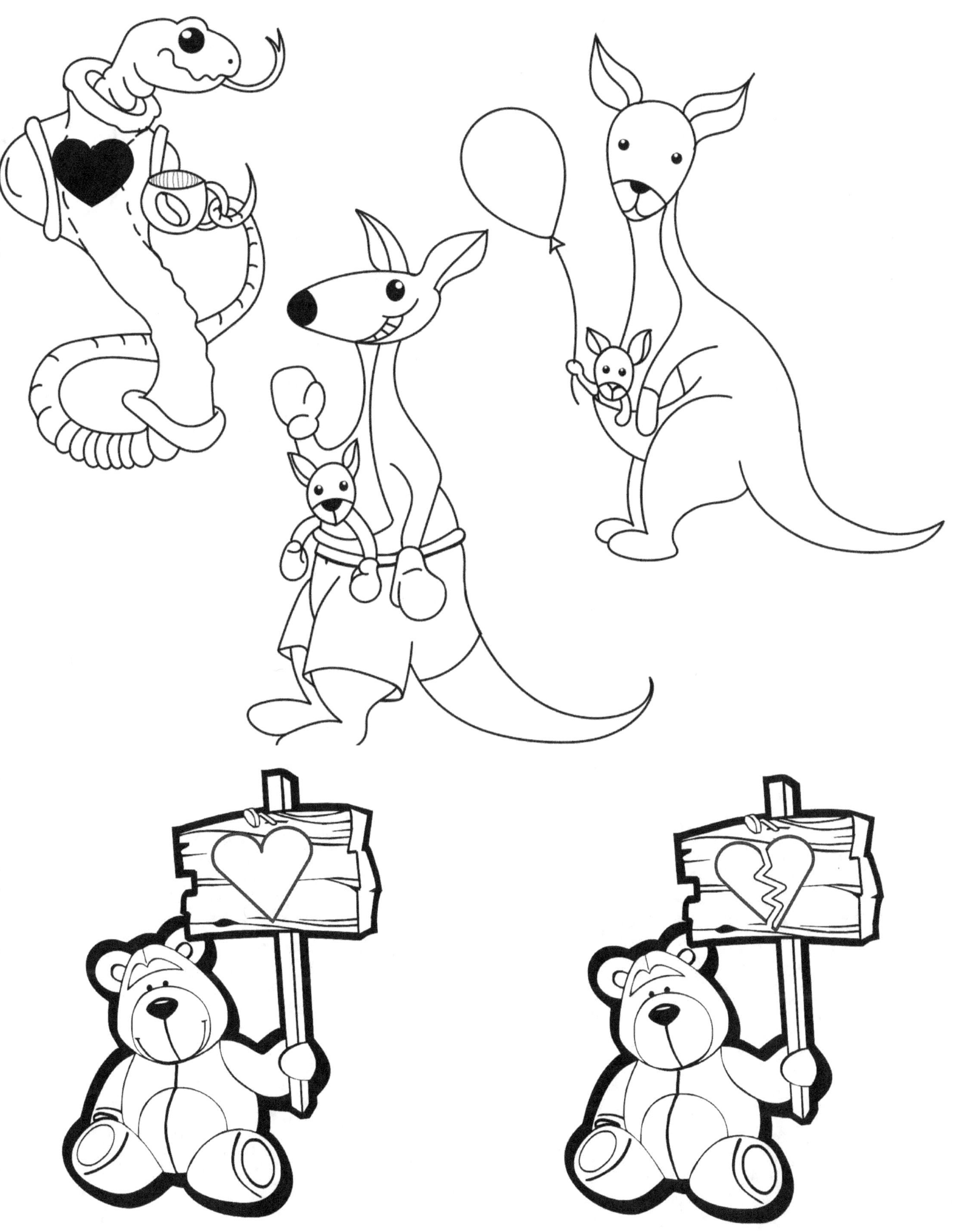

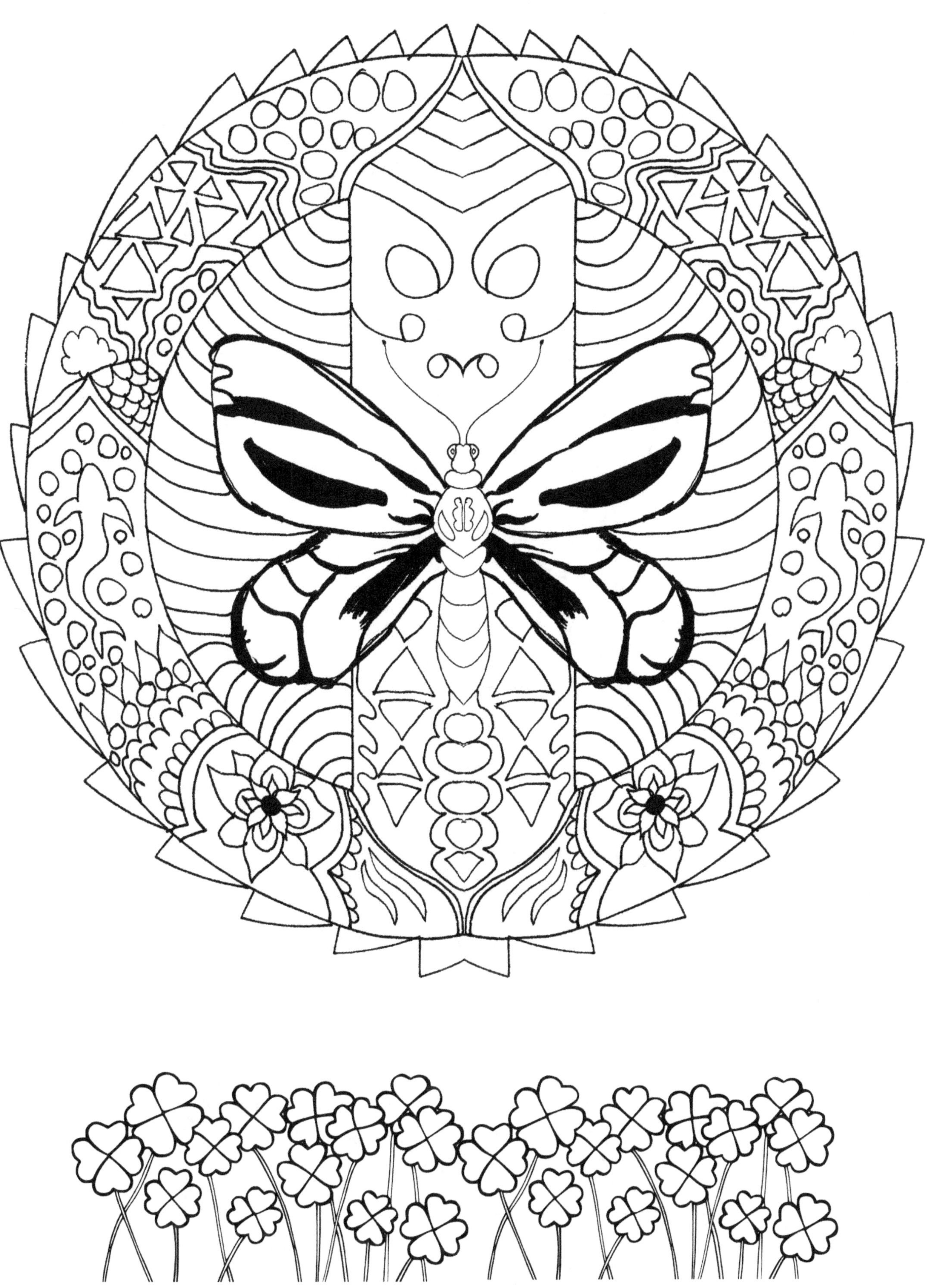

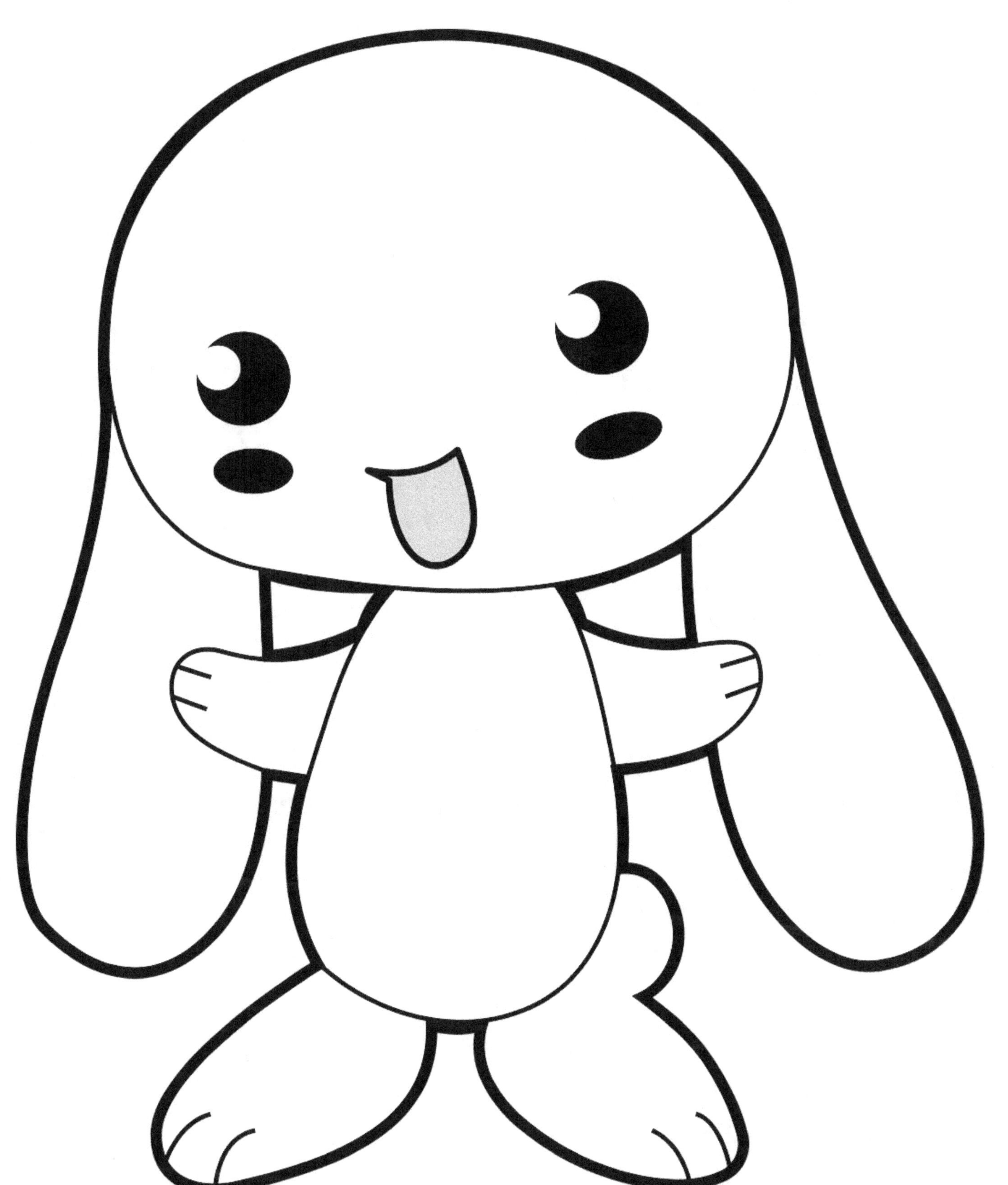

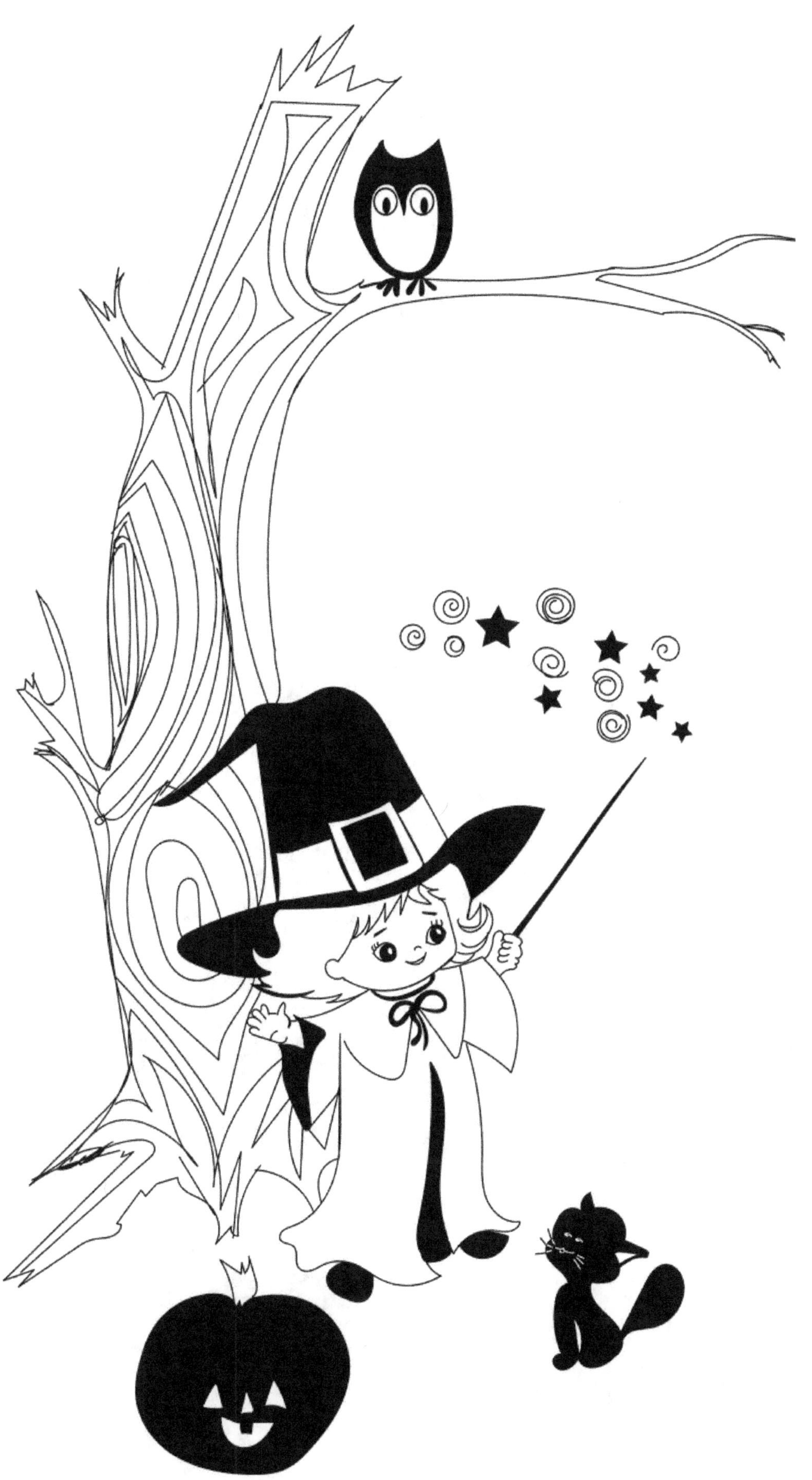

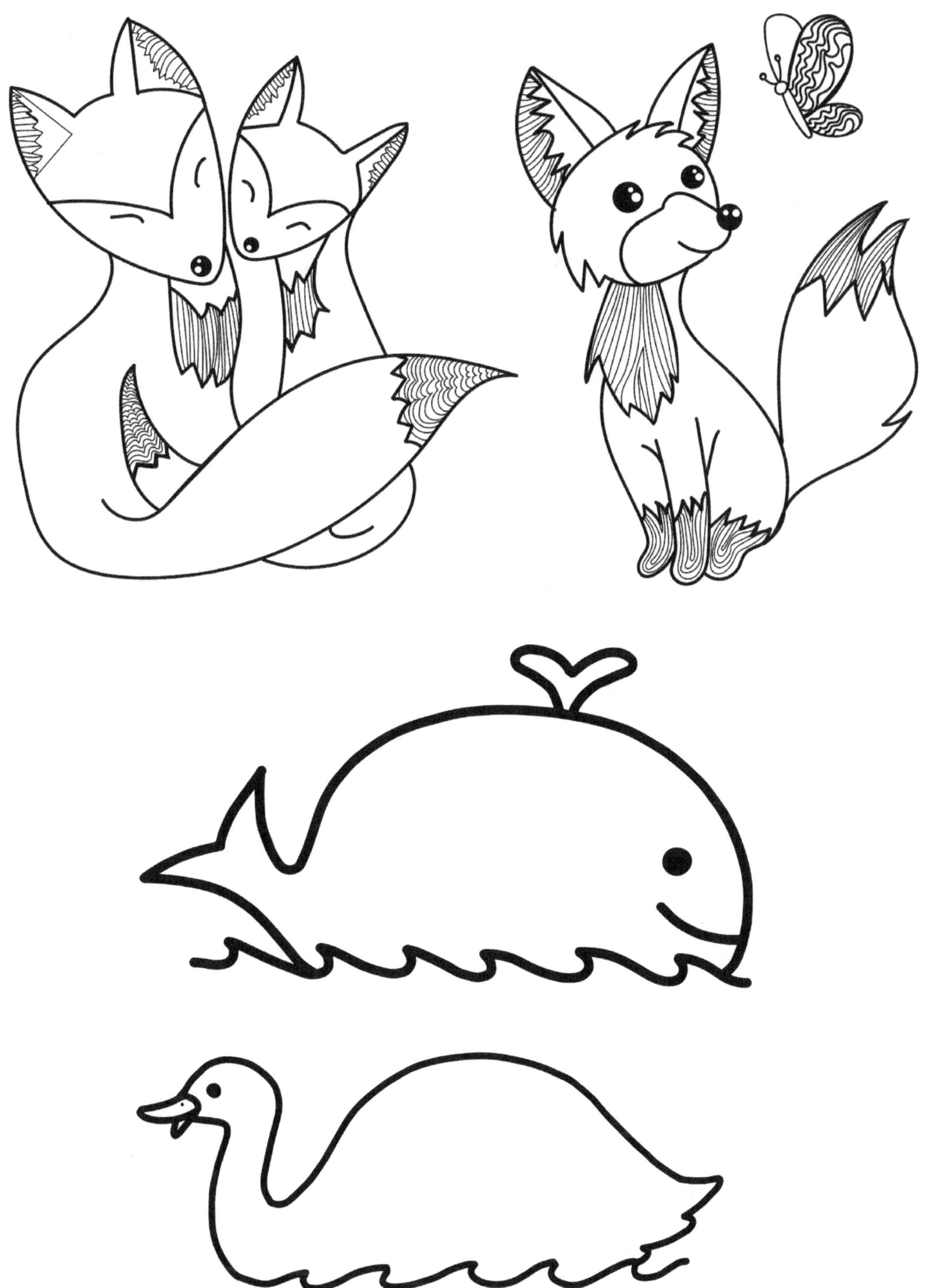

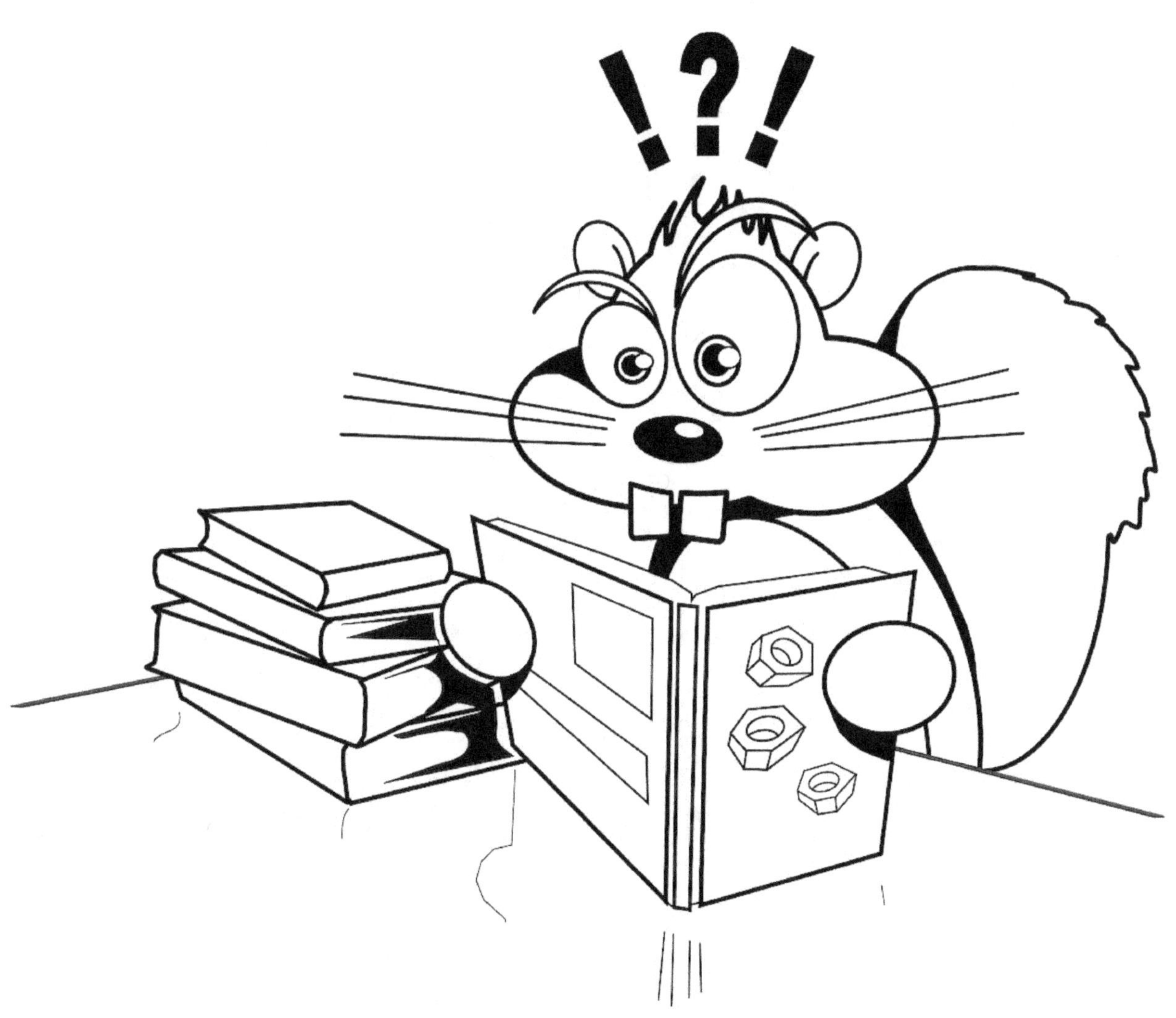

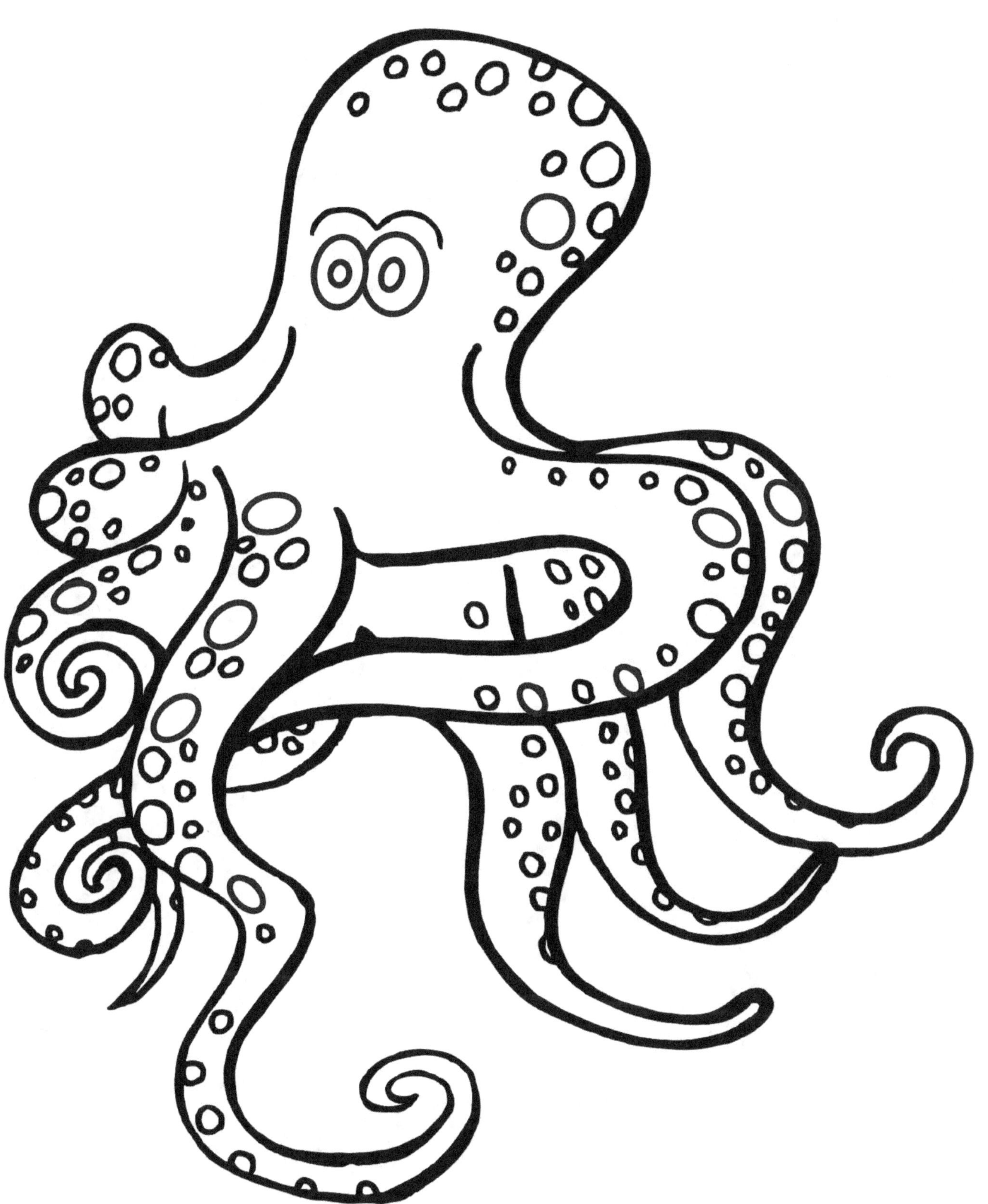

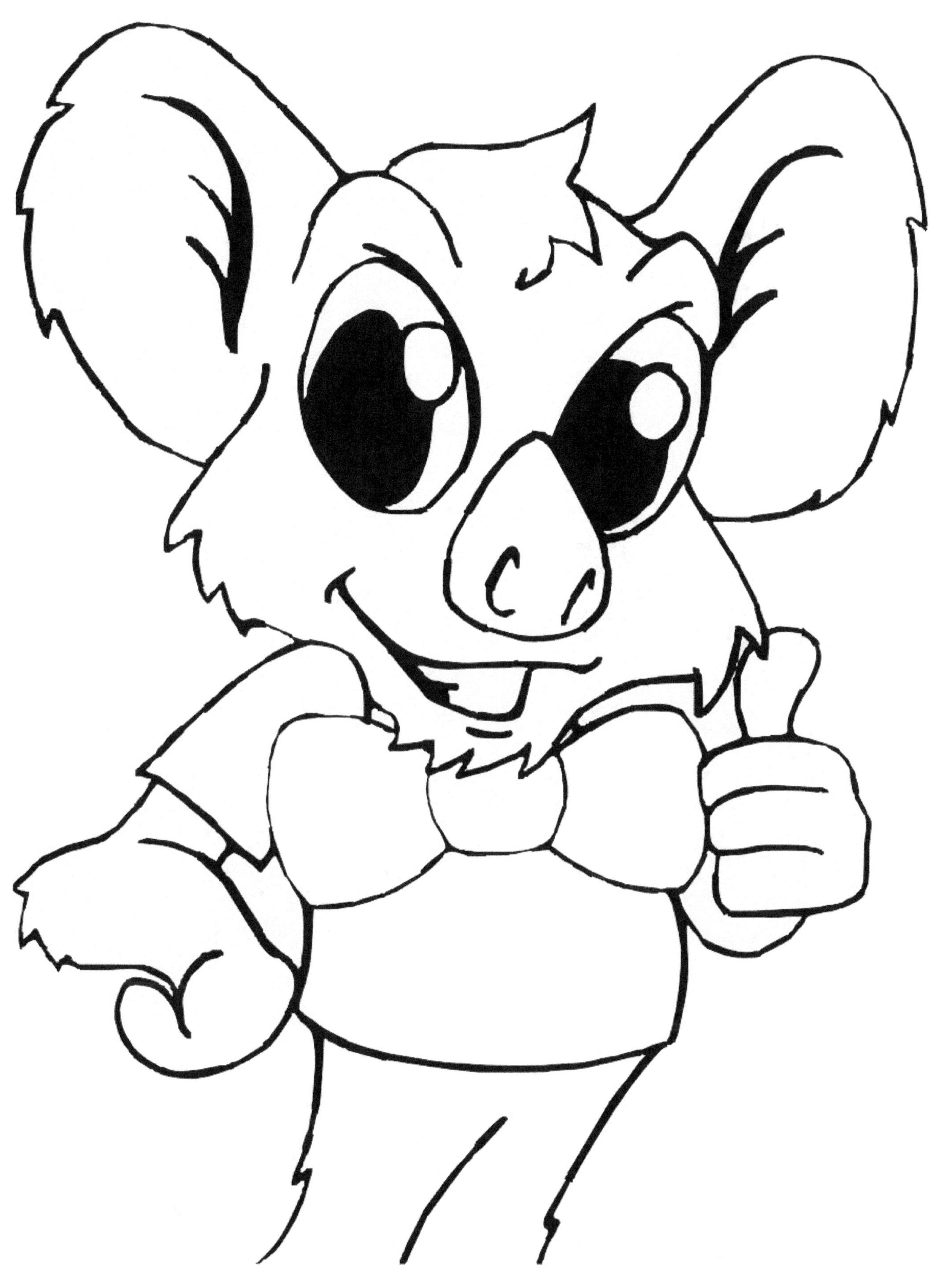

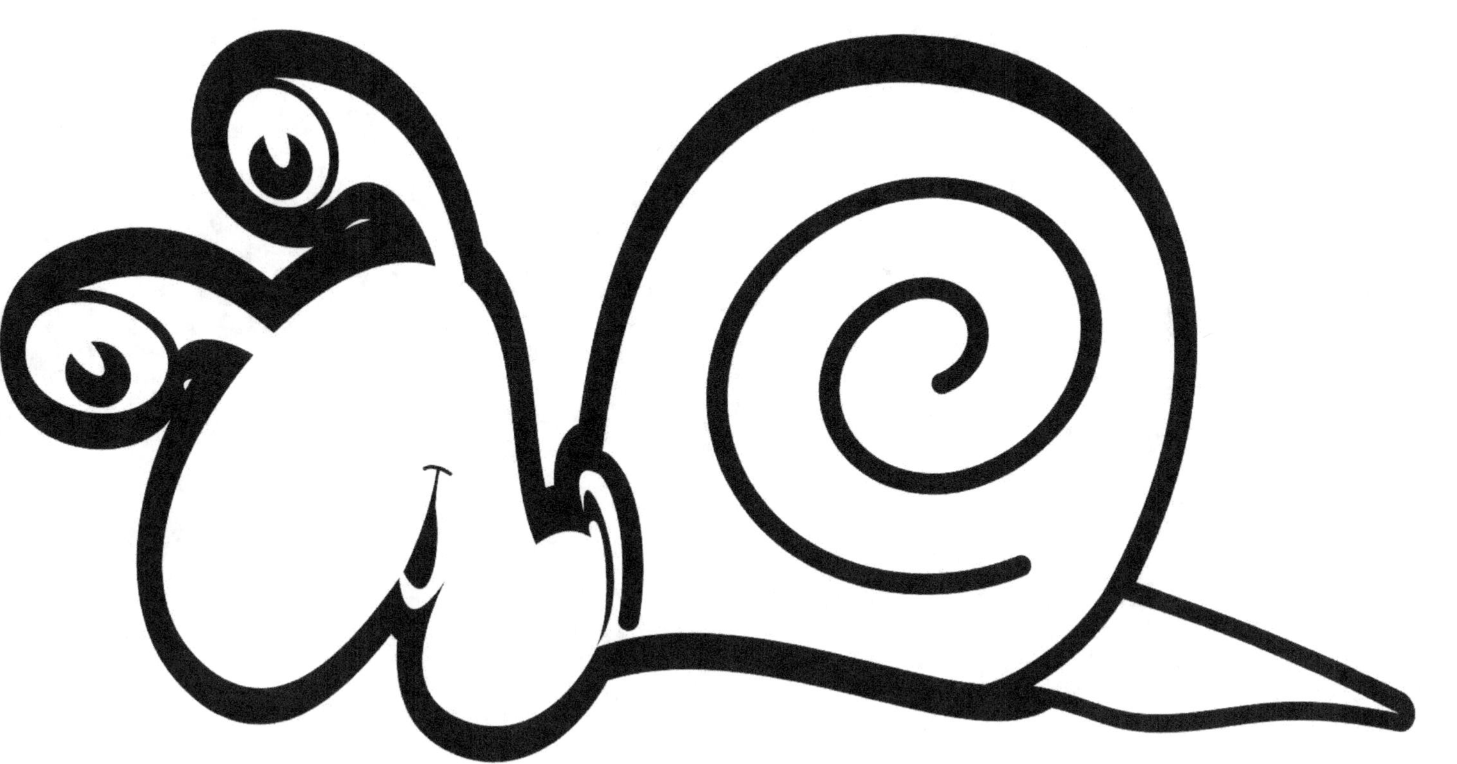

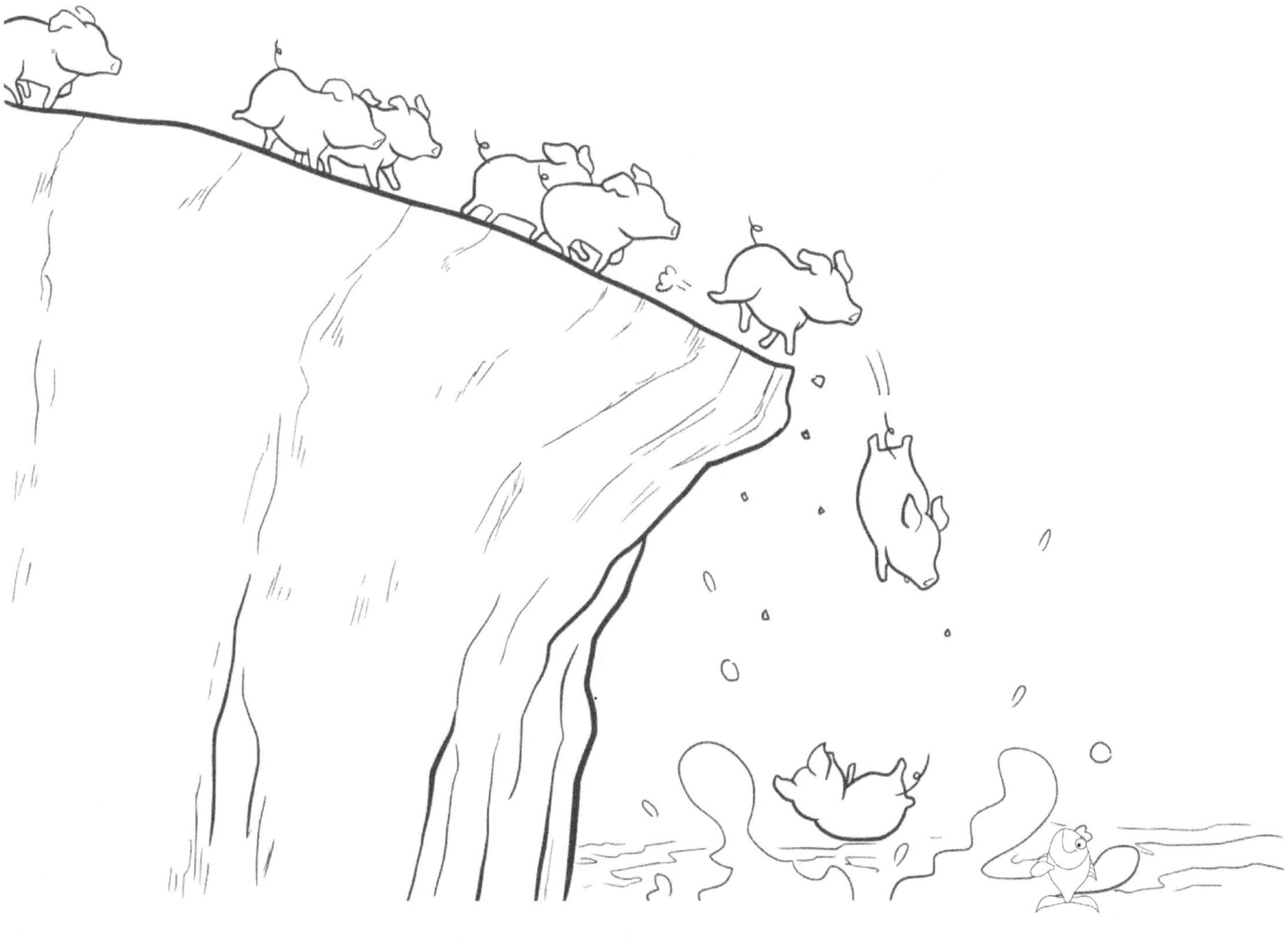

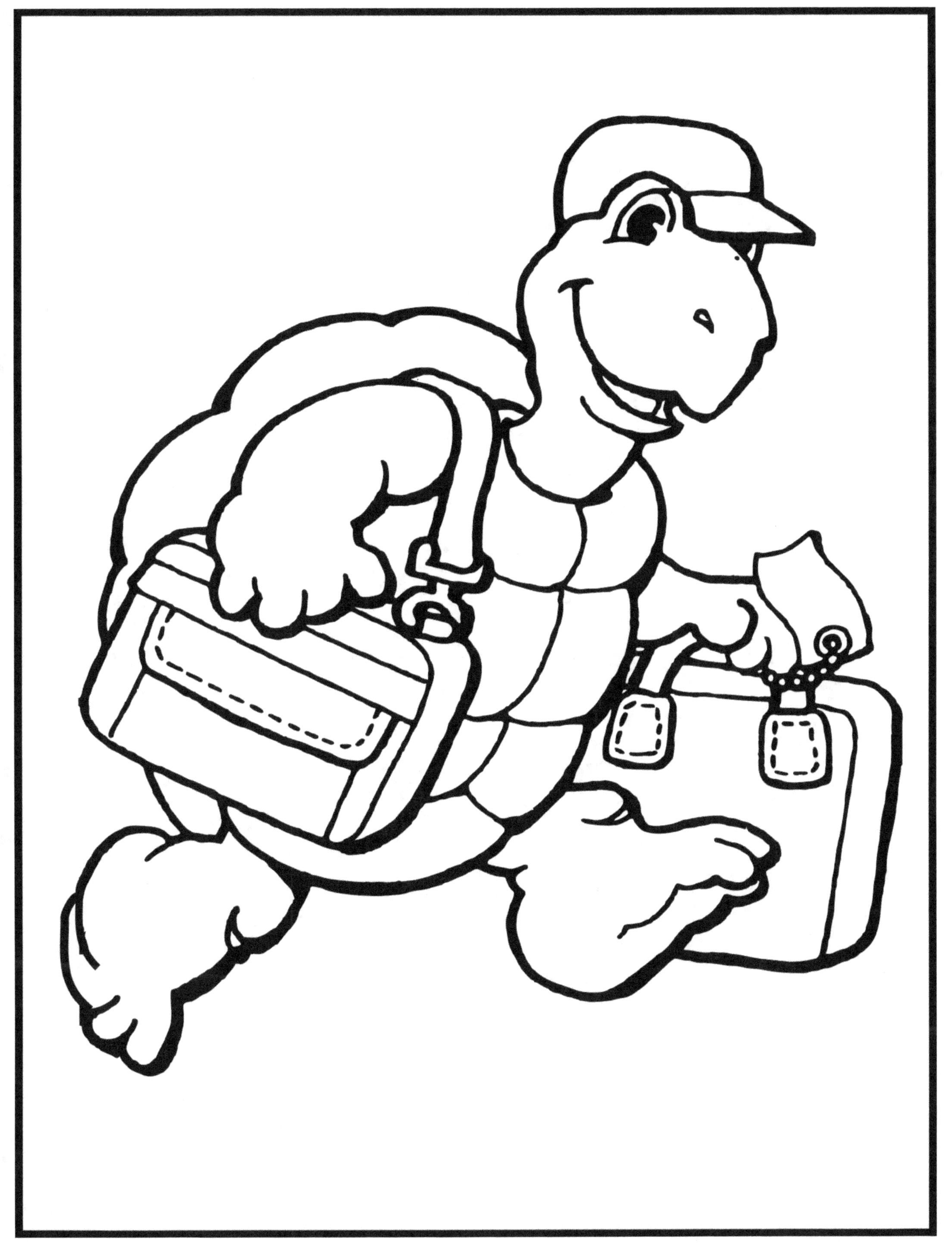

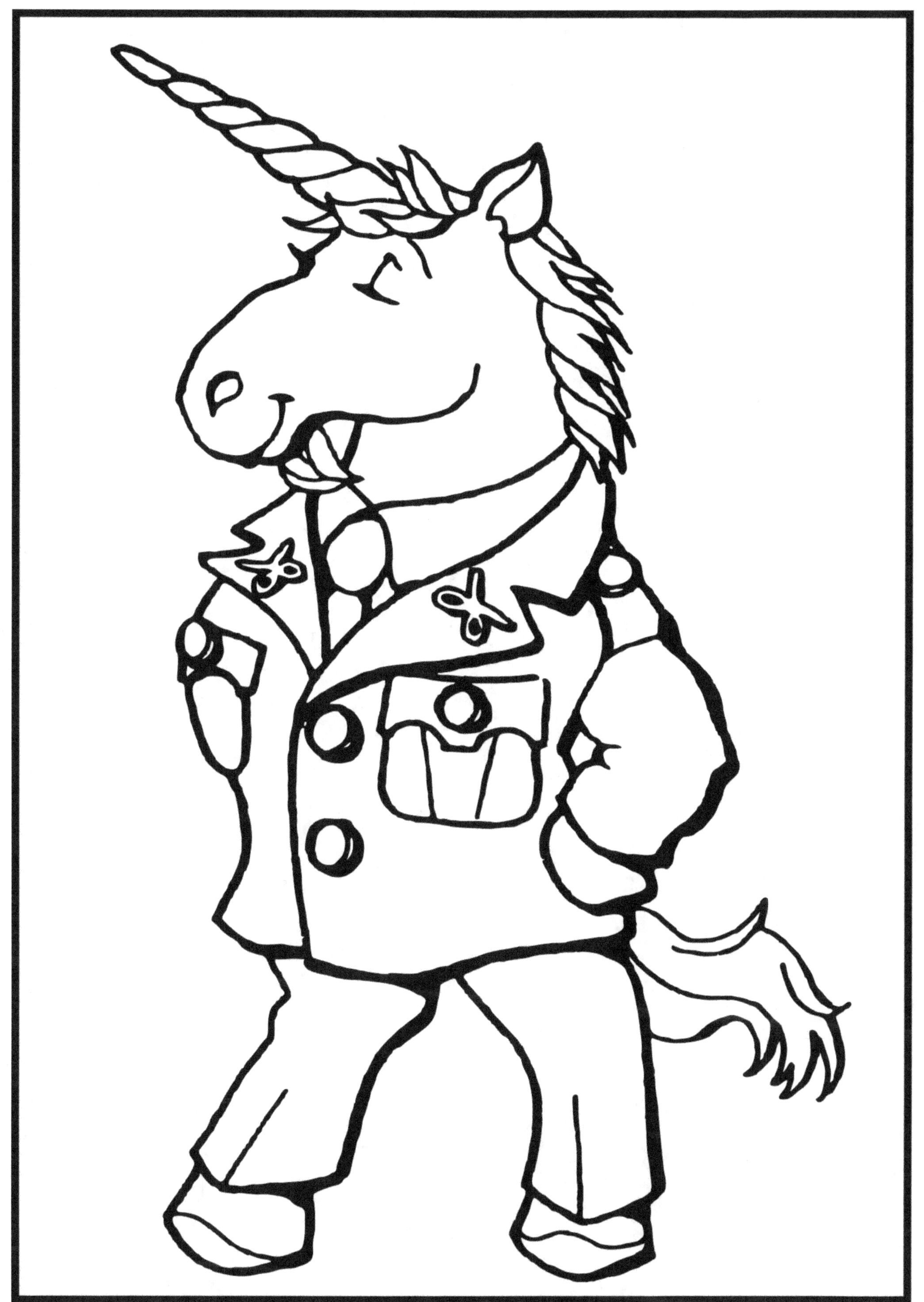

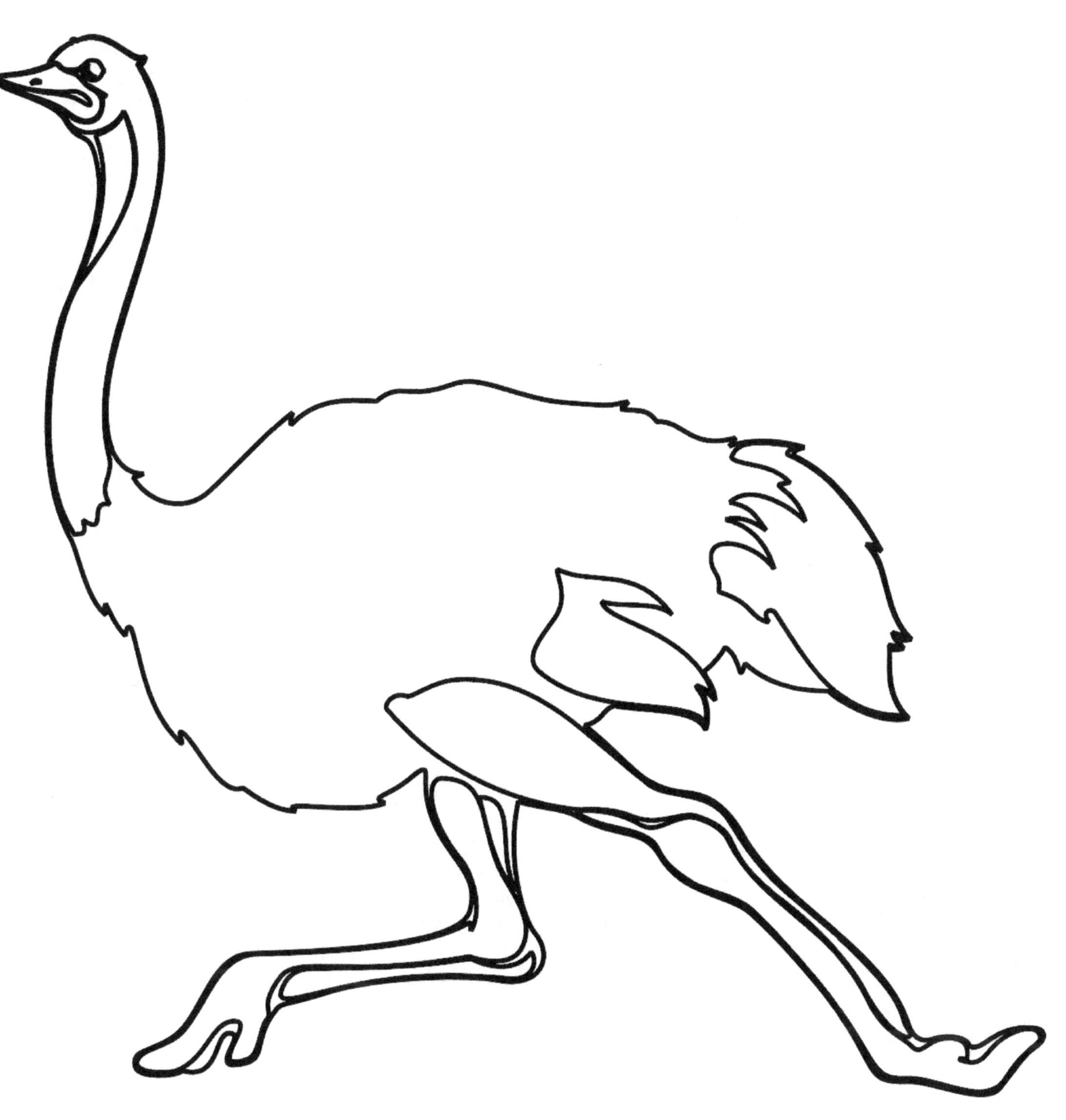

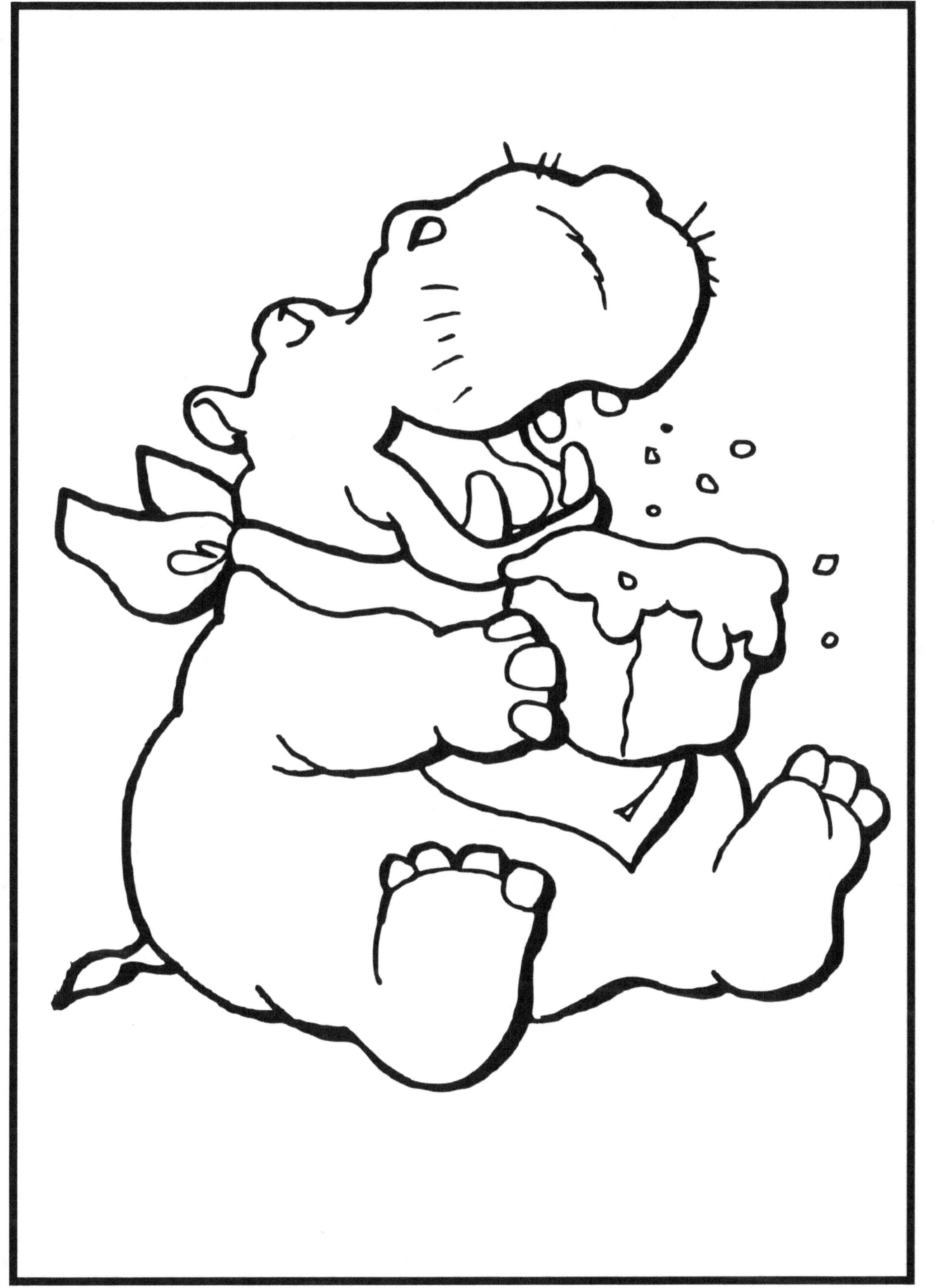

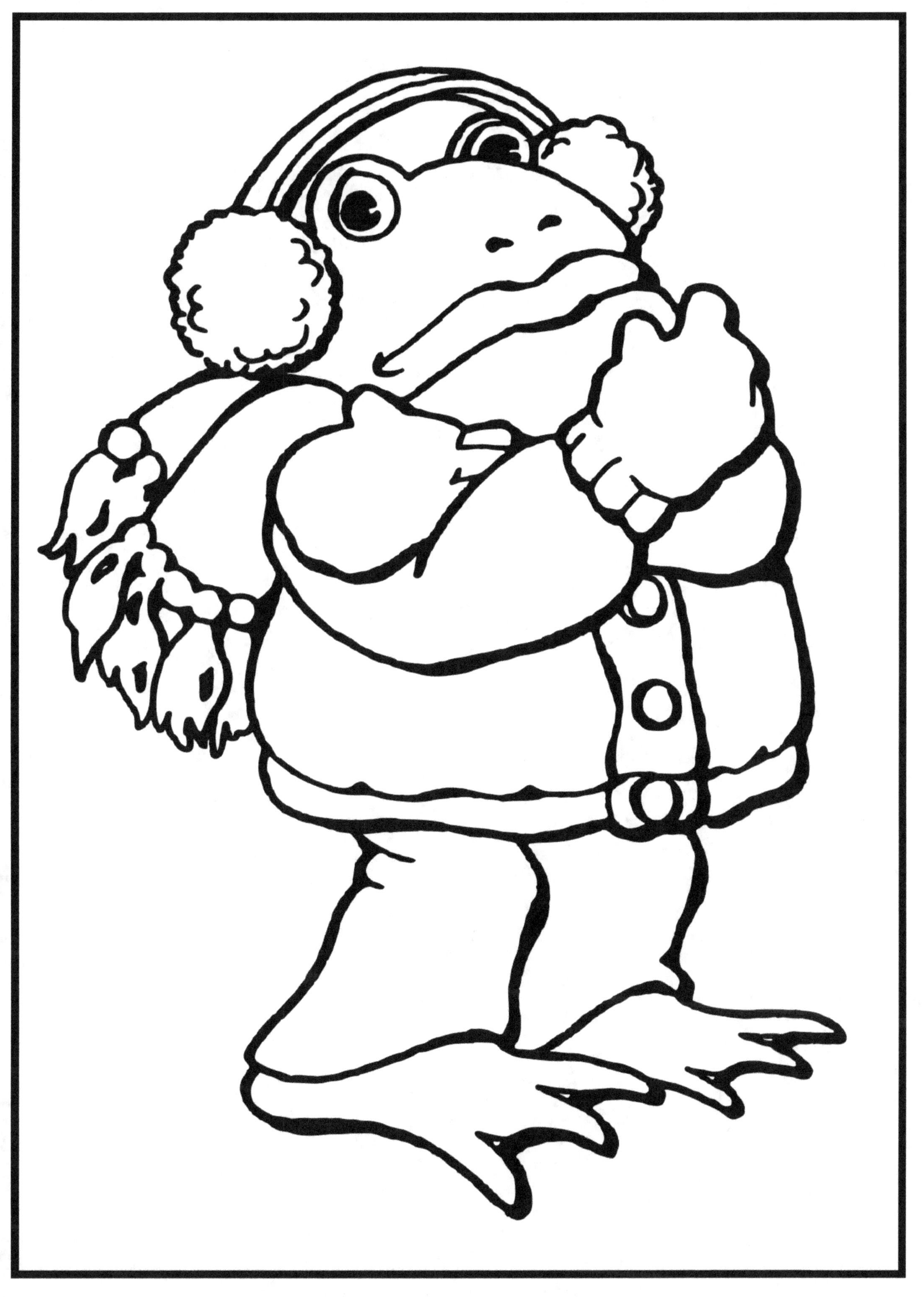

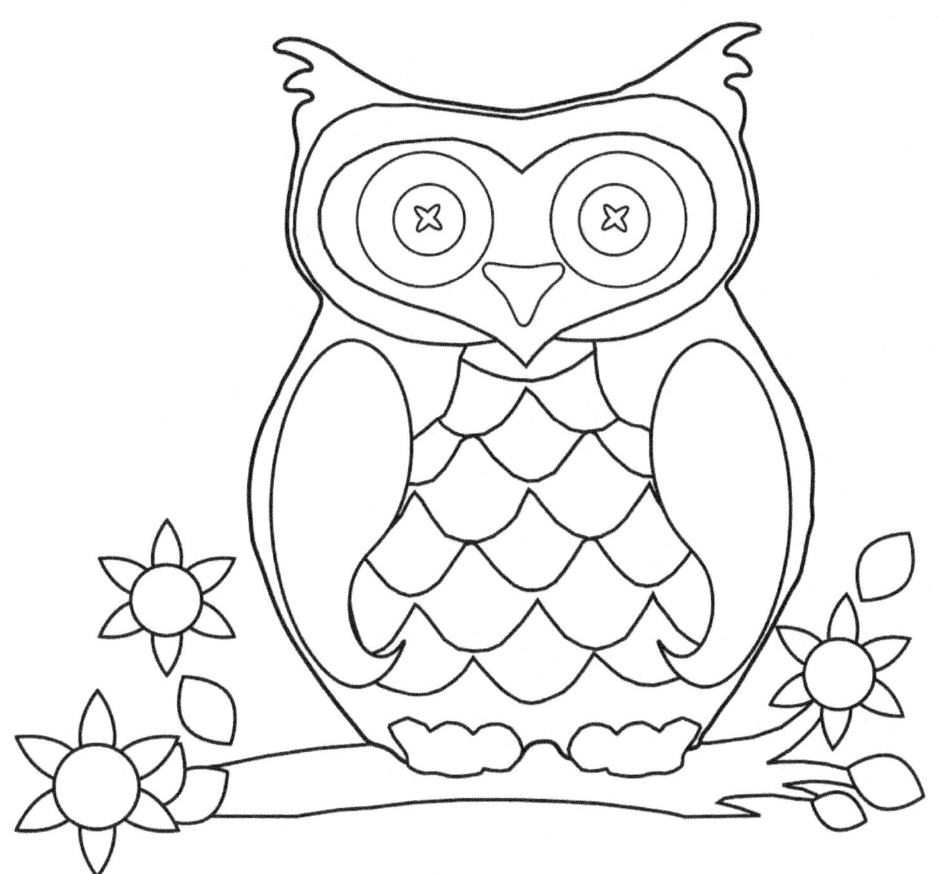

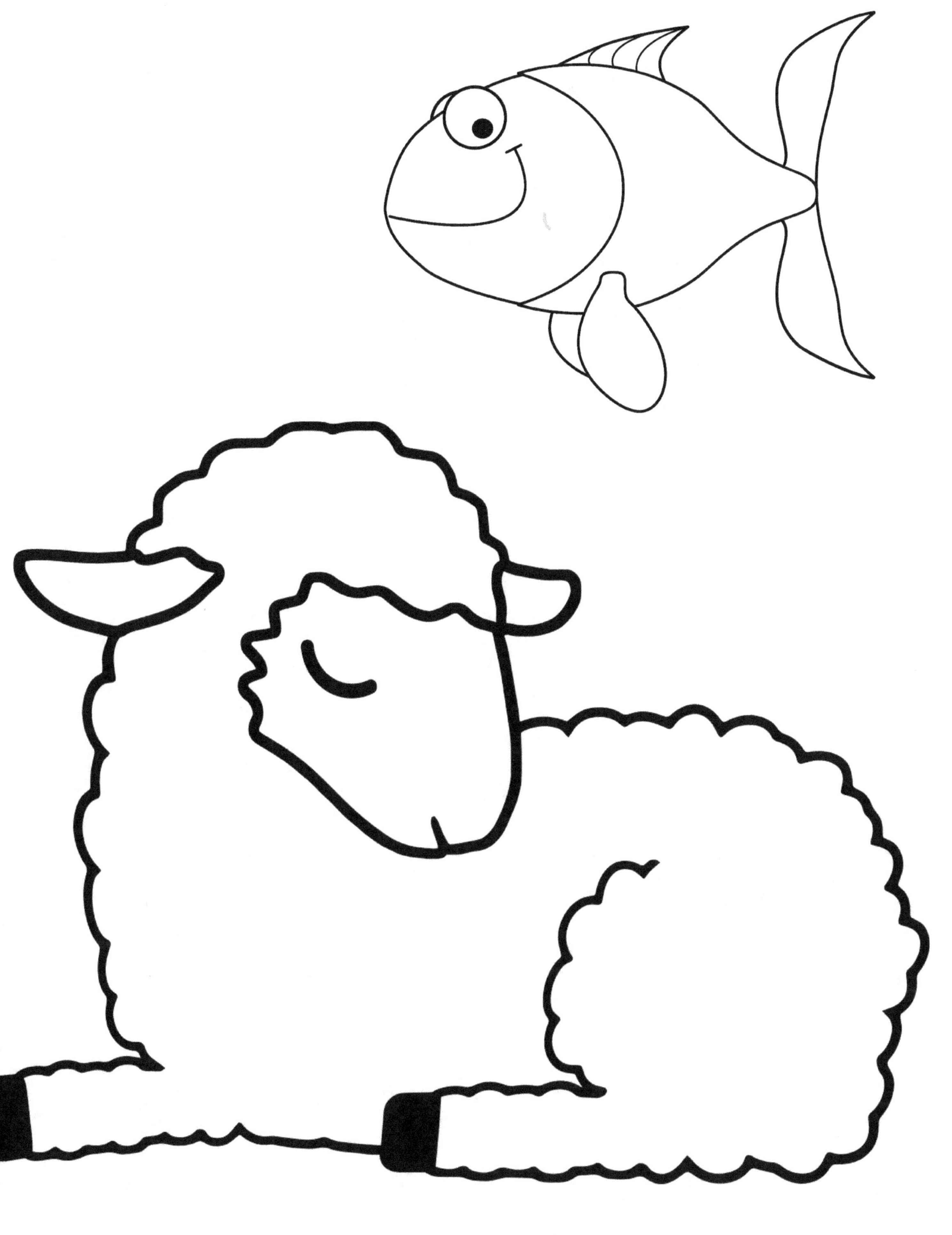

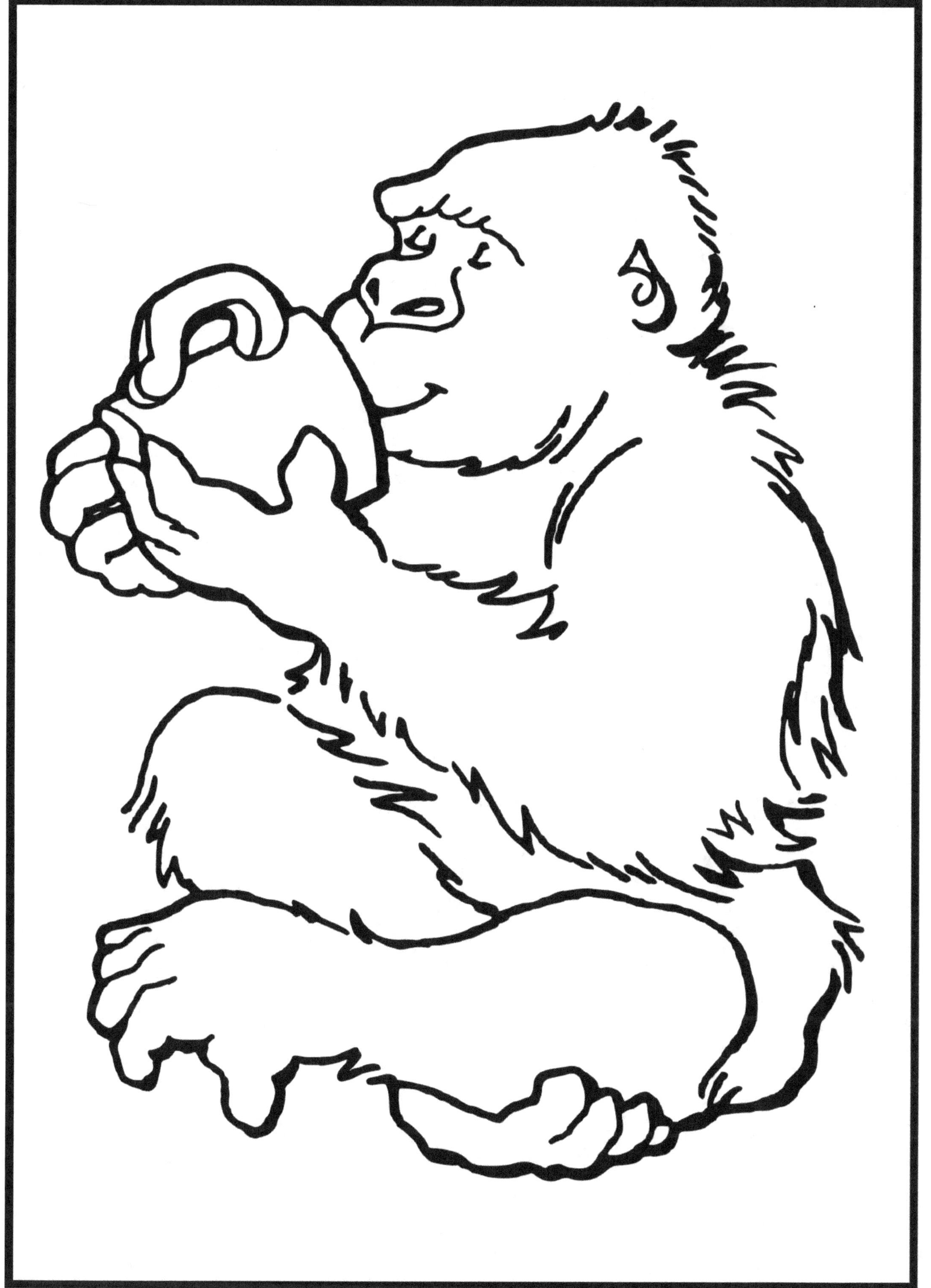

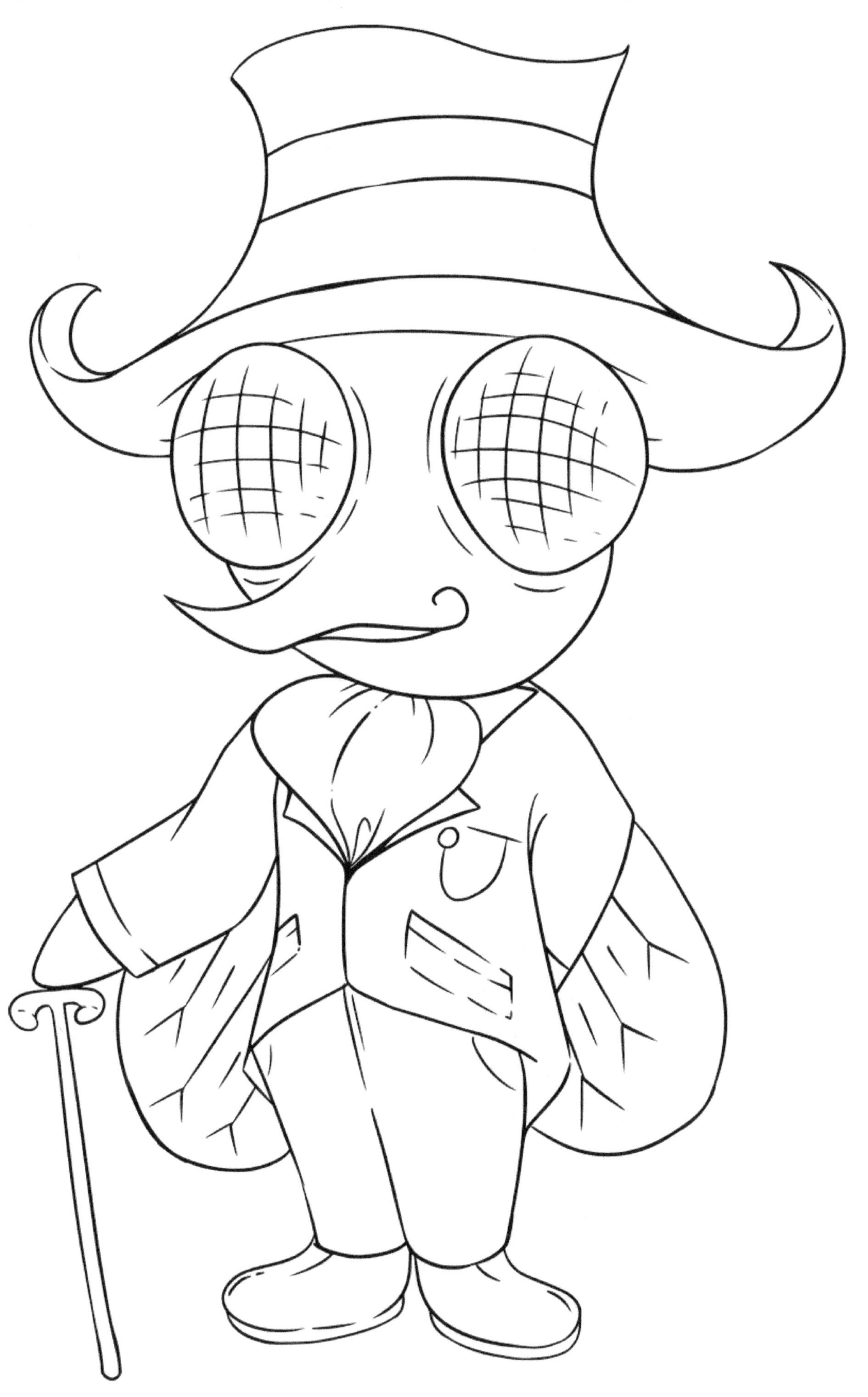

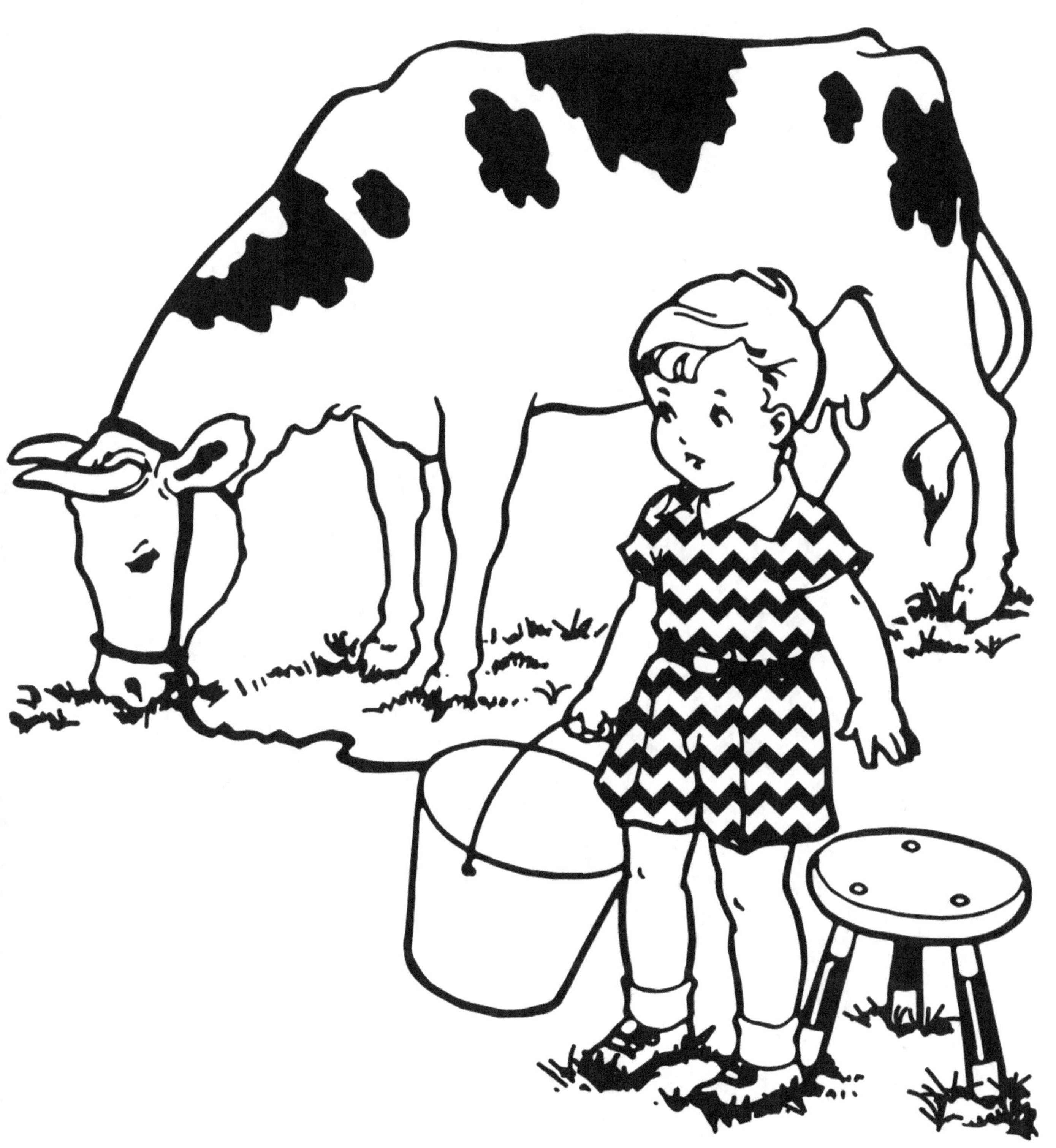

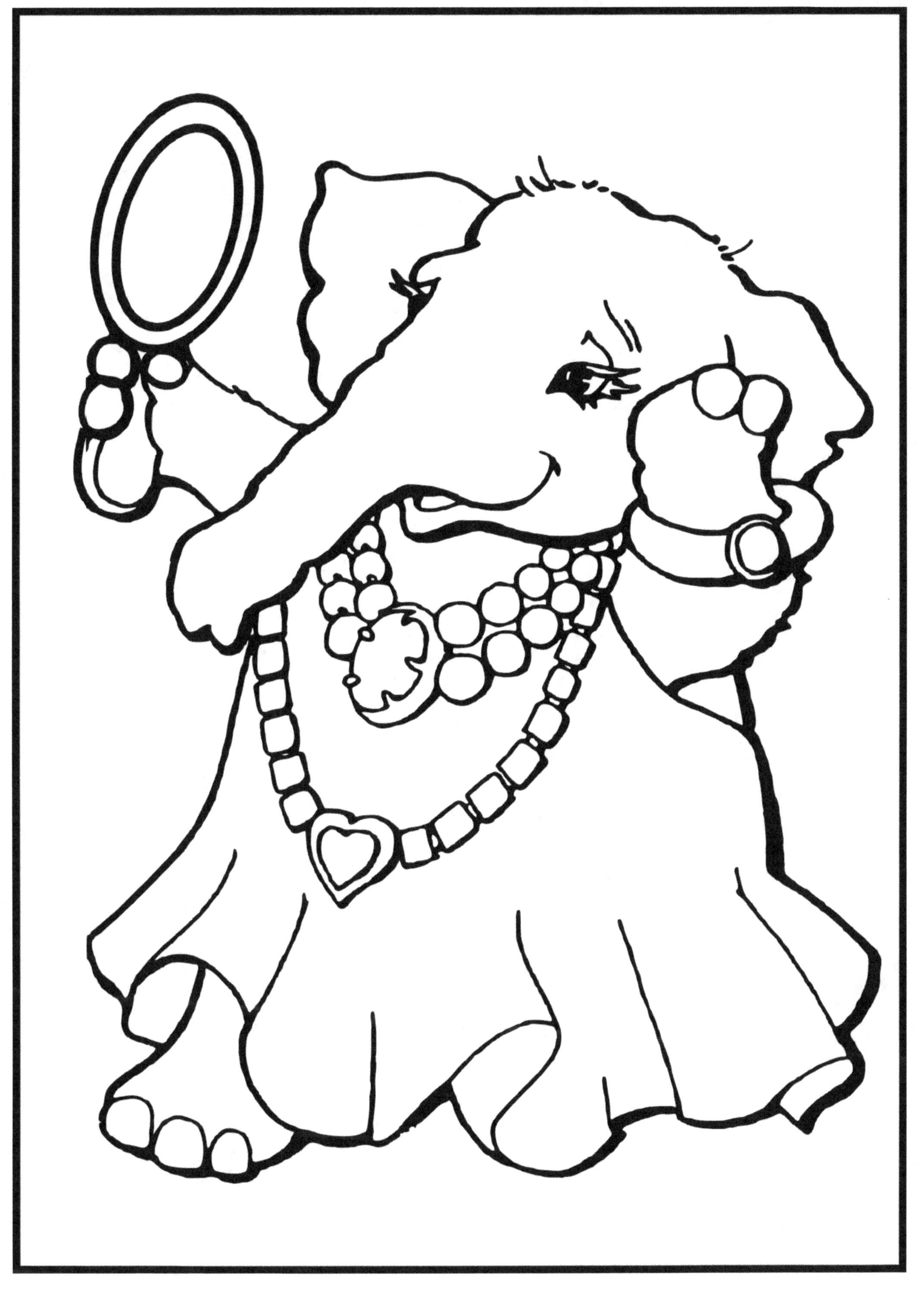

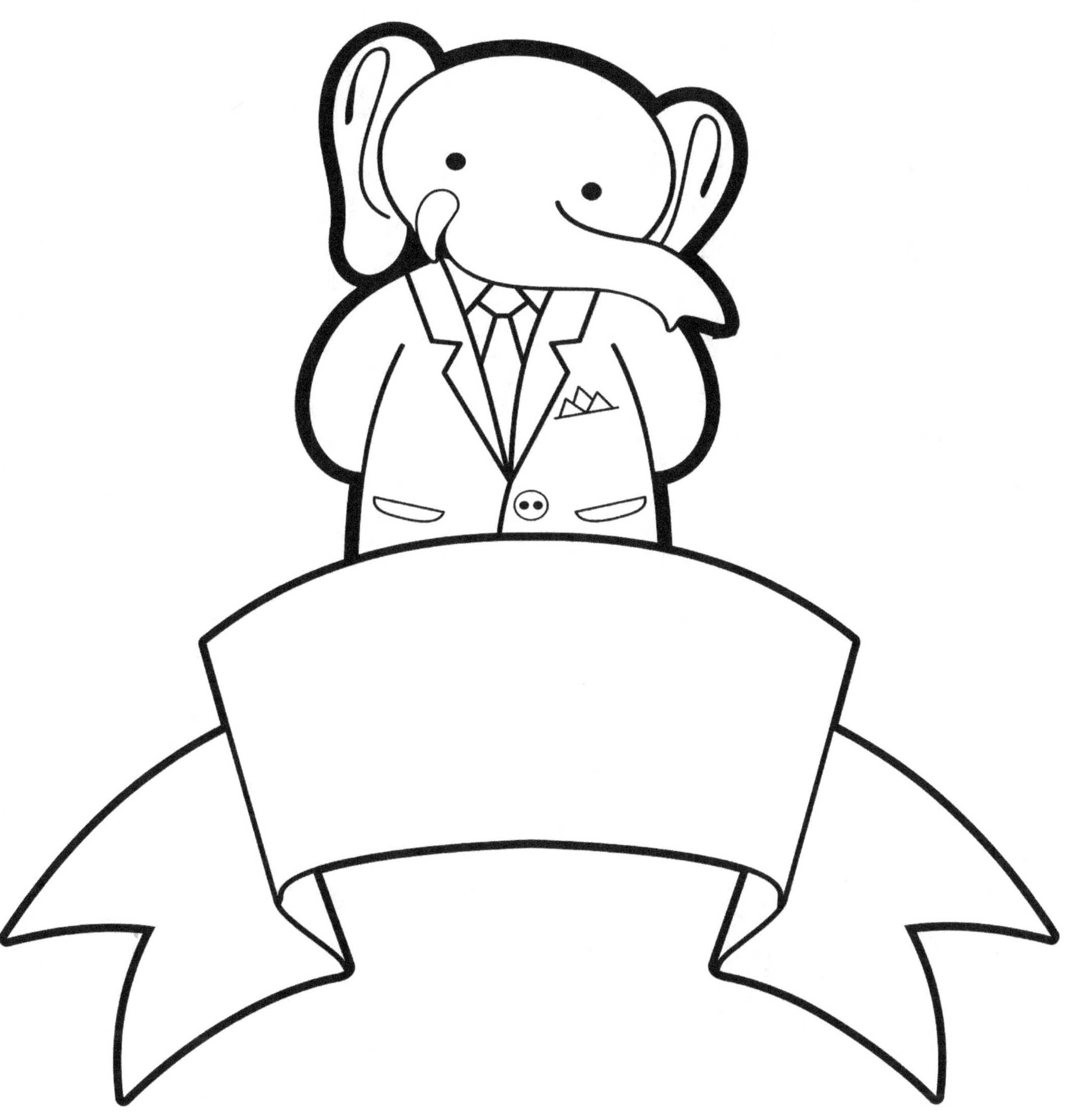

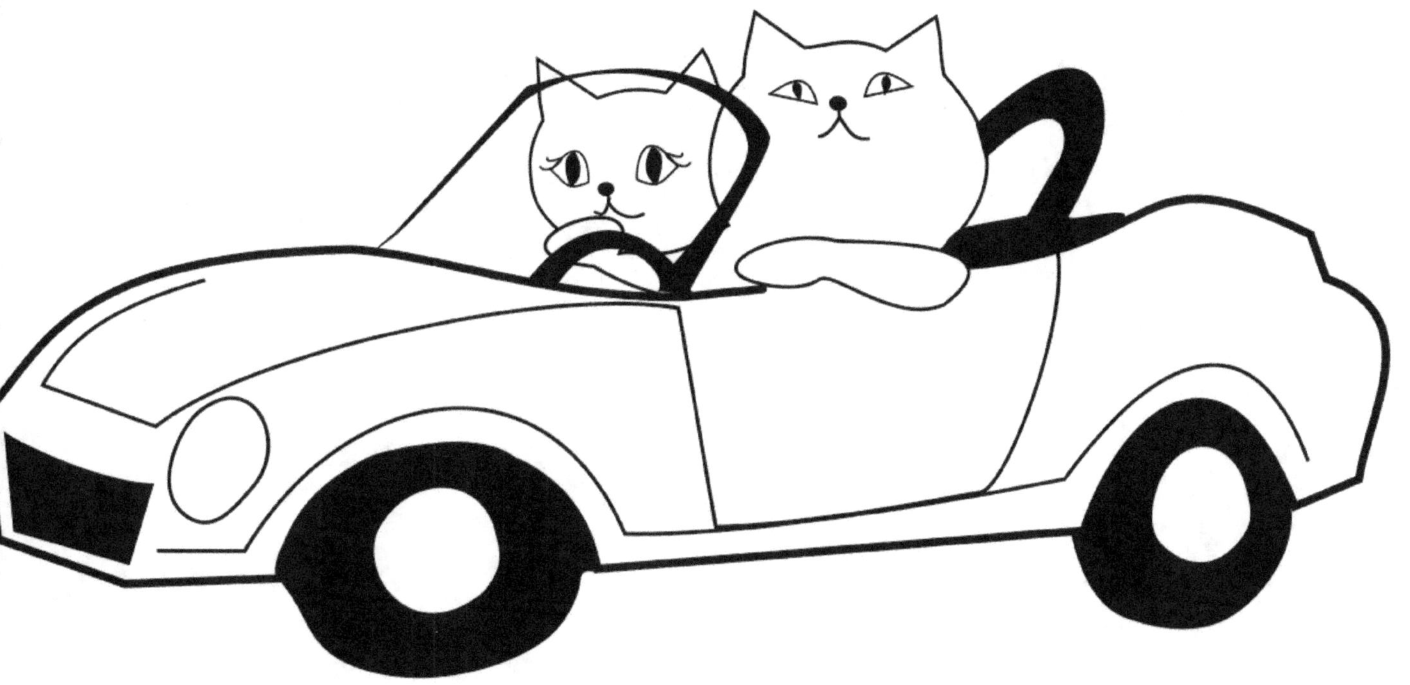

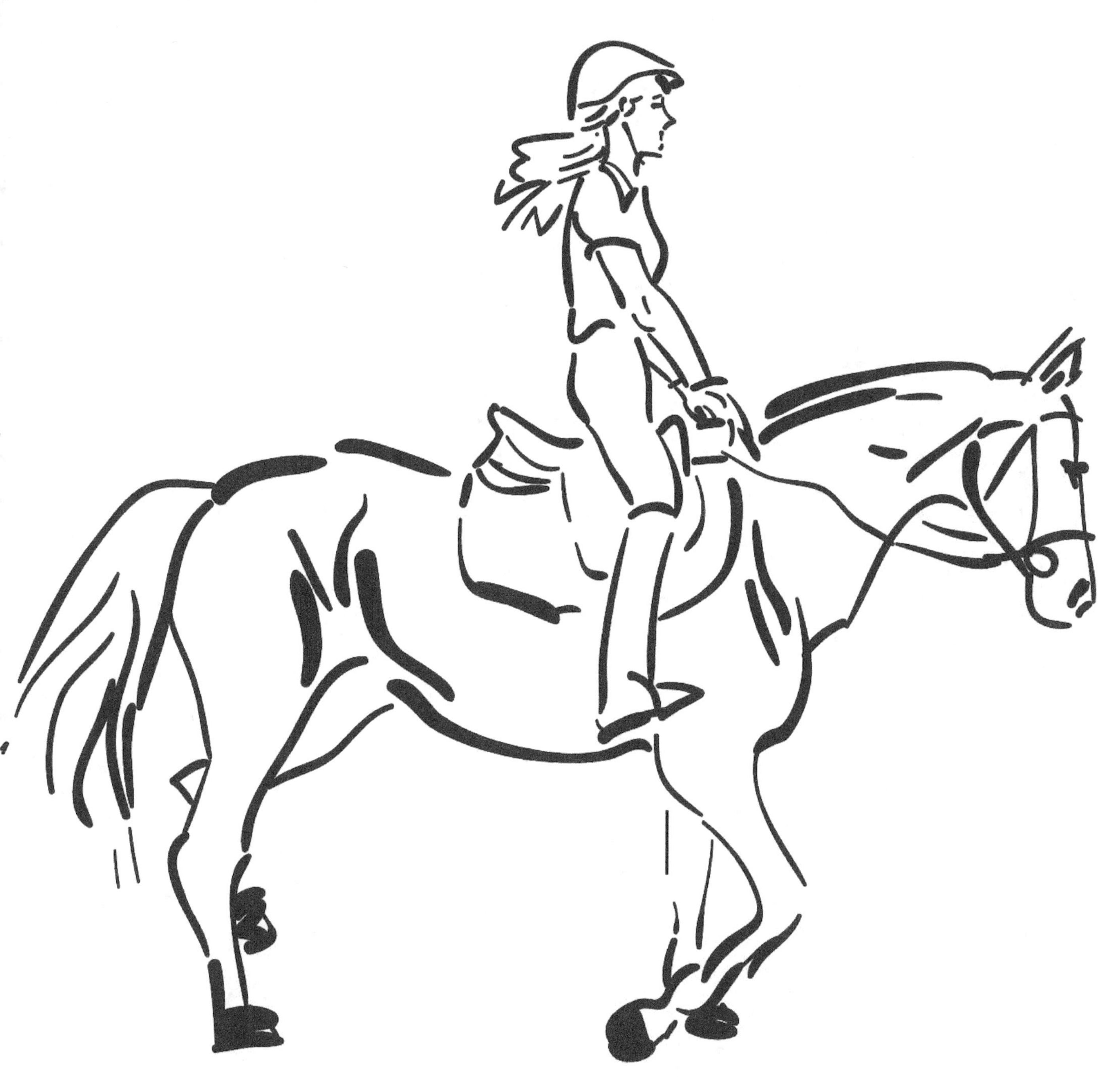

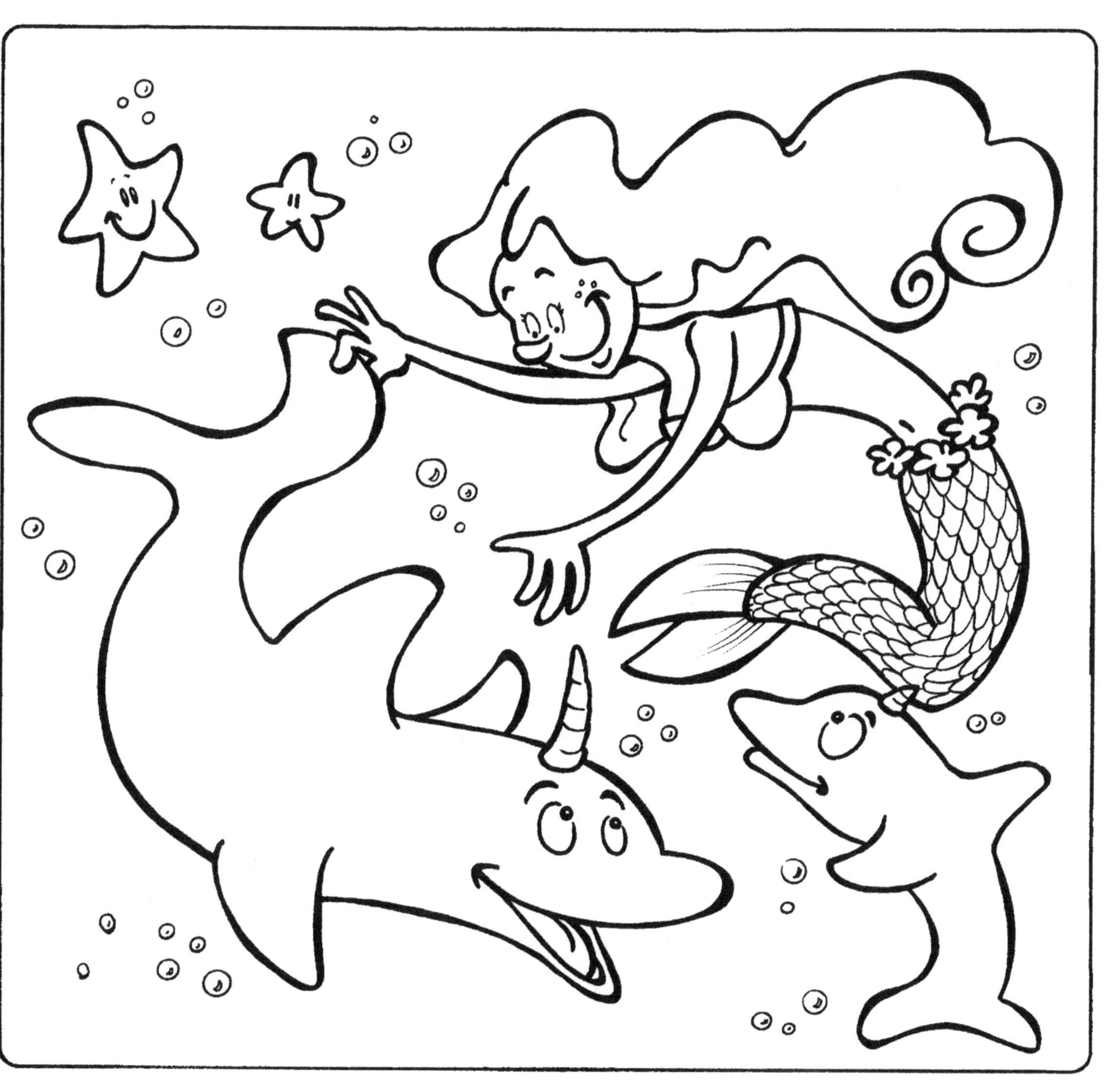

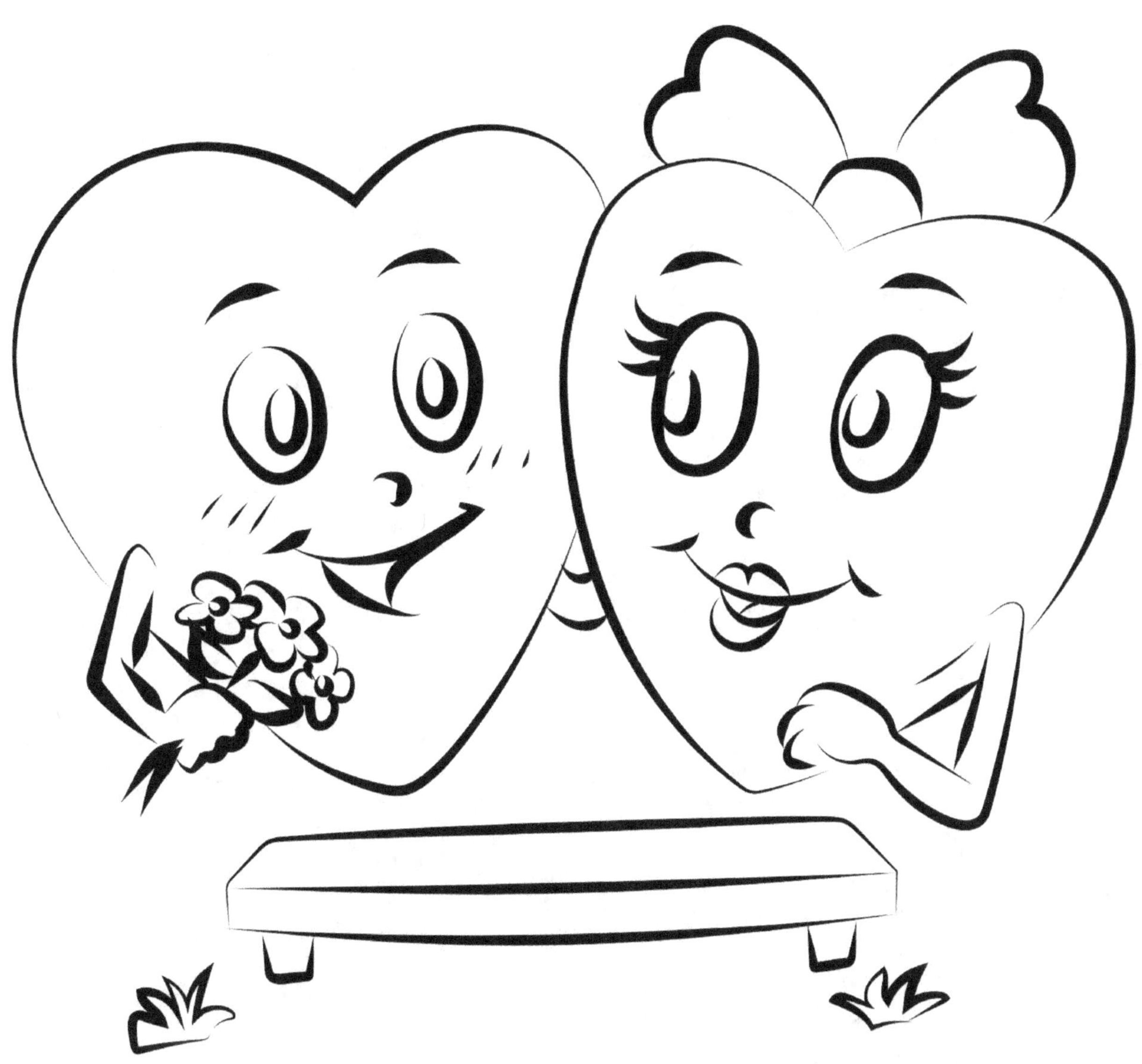

www.ingramcontent.com/pod-product-compliance
Lightning Source LLC
Chambersburg PA
CBHW081359160726
48000CB00010B/3405

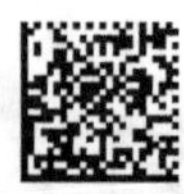
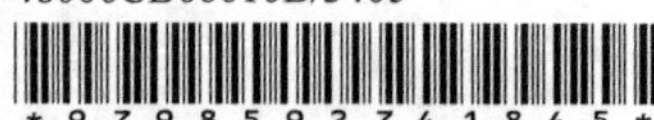